Come ....

Why wouldn't it need to be precise? Mine will be precise.
—Matthew to John, Ep. 1A

Speaking of broken bones, what's the story?
—Jesus to Melech, Ep. 1B

Once you've met the Messiah, "am" is all that matters.
—Philip to Matthew, Ep. 2

What is happening? What are we a part of?
—Thomas to the other disciples, Ep. 3

Sometimes you've got to stir up the water.
—Jesus to Peter, John and Matthew, Ep. 4

It's becoming real isn't it? Everything we prepared for.
—John the Baptist to Jesus, Ep. 5

Did you really think that you'd never struggle or sin again?
—Jesus to Mary Magdalene, Ep. 6

Jesus of Nazareth, we finally meet.
—Quintus to Jesus, Ep. 7

I'm not here to be sentimental and soothing.
—Jesus to Matthew, Ep. 8

The Chosen Study

Hope for the Lost

The Chosen Study

Hope for the Lost

A welcoming and
Interactive experience for everyone:
observers... skeptics... learners... seekers... followers.

The Chosen Study Team

Bill & Teresa Syrios, Dietrich Gruen,
Tori Foss, Bill Ditewig and Don & Cathy Baker

TheChosenStudy.org
Watch > Discover > Relate
the Most Audascious
Story ever told.

Those who hope in the L<small>ORD</small> will renew their strength.
They will soar on wings like eagles; they will run and not grow weary;
they will walk and not be faint.
-Isaiah 40:31

Crossover Press

©2022 The Chosen Study: Season Two, Bill Syrios & TCS Team

Scripture quotations are from the ESV® Bible (The Holy Bible, English Standard Version®), ©2001 by Crossway, a publishing ministry of Good News Publishers. Used by permission. All rights reserved.

The Chosen Study is not affiliated with The Chosen TV show or Angel Studios.

ISBN: 978-0-9716683-4-8

"**The Chosen** is a television drama based on the life of Jesus Christ, created directed and co-written by American filmmaker, Dallas Jenkins. It is the first multi-season series about the life of Christ, and season one was the highest crowd-funded TV series or film project of all time.

The series' creators stated that they had hoped to distinguish the new series from previous portrayals of Jesus by crafting a multi-season episode-based story. The series portrays Jesus 'through the eyes of those who met him.'"   –*The Chosen*, Wikipedia

The Chosen Study focuses on *filling out* the series with Scripture passages to take everyone deeper. The guide can profitably be used by individuals with the hope that they... we... facilitate outreach and learning with others in one-on-one and group contexts. After all: *People must know!*

Contents

Welcome to The Chosen Study: Season Two

Like the man himself, the accounts of Jesus' life and ministry are unique in the field of literature. Ancient writings include historical accounts, personal memoirs, and mythological stories. But none of these styles describe how Matthew, Mark, Luke, and John wrote.

They combine the roles of historian, biographer, theologian, and pastor. These "reporters" are not simply neutral observers but men who had been deeply influenced by the message they desired to communicate. Lacking literary precedent, second-century Christians called them *Evangelists,* and their writings, *The Gospels.*

The English word "gospel" comes from the Greek term, *evangelion,* which means "good news." The four Evangelists wanted their readers to not only know how remarkable Jesus was, but to know how good his message becomes in the lives of those who embrace it.

To understand that message better, we have selected key Bible passages portrayed in *The Chosen.* So, wherever you may be spiritually— an **observer… skeptic… learner… seeker… or follower**—we're glad you've joined in to learn from those who knew Jesus best.

Bible Study 2.0 = Food + Film + Scripture + Discussion

The Chosen Study includes ten studies. We typically:

–**Meet weekly** to watch>discover>relate and to develop friendships.

–**Start with a meal,** potluck, or finger food to relax with each other.

–**Have no need** to bring Bibles. This guide includes all Scripture used.

–**Share** at our comfort level. No one is asked to sing, pray or read aloud.

–**Are facilitated** by a leader who guides group discussion and pace.

Where to Meet

Churches are convenient because they have kitchens, tables and are free, but also look for non-church, friendly alternatives like hotel conference or community rooms, homes, colleges, offices, and cafés.

Size Options: How large is your group? (See also page 146.)

| One-on-One Get-Togethers | or | Small Group Meetings | or | Small/Large (8+) Group Gatherings |

Time Options: How much time do you have?

Longer: WATCH > DISCOVER > RELATE with food as set out in this guide takes *2½ to 3 hours*. **This format is most impactful and cited below.** *

Medium: If limited to *1½ to 2 hours*, you will need to skip questions or just read the first Discover section to condense and keep up the pace.

Shorter: If the group has less time, say *an hour*, you could: 1) watch the episode and, 2) study the passages before coming. Then as you meet, you would discuss what you watched / studied in preparation. (This option is less than ideal if members' preparation is inconsistent.)

Note: All studies have a WATCH section. Studies #2, #3, #4, #6, #7, and #8 include two passages and TWO DISCOVER sections. If you are short on time, you could ask the group to study the first passage on their own and then study the second passage together.

#1, #5, #9, and #10 have one WATCH and one DISCOVER section: WATCH > DISCOVER > RELATE. Always plan on pacing yourselves to leave adequate time for the RELATE section at end of each study.

*EXAMPLE: Midweek Evening	*EXAMPLE: Saturday Morning
5:45 ARRIVE: 15 min. to gather	**8:45 ARRIVE:** 15 min. to gather
6:00 POTLUCK: 30 min. to relax/eat	**9:00 LITE BREAKFAST:** 15 min.
6:30-8:45 *THE CHOSEN STUDY*	**9:15-11:30 *THE CHOSEN STUDY***

Guide Overview

The Chosen Study Guide provides a means of bringing people together to study and discuss Chosen episodes with Scripture. This framework gives direction to a wide variety of group studies and discussions:

How to Lead the Study

Tips to help current (and future) leaders prepare
Please read pages 18-19 thoroughly.

FROM **The** **CHOSEN**

WATCH *View Episode Together > Discuss*

Questions that take us deeper into the episode.

FROM **The** **BIBLE**

DISCOVER *Read Text > Mark Up > Discuss*

Intro/"Look Fors"/Questions for passage's meaning.

RELATE *Apply Insights to God / Life / You > Discuss*

Personal questions that help us apply the passage in our lives.

*Next two sections are for reference, not to discuss, unless time allows.**

NOTES on the Study *Commentary and Historical Context*

The biblical passages' context and meaning put into perspective.

REALISTIC **But** **REAL?**

That's plausible but did it happen?

The Chosen's artistic license put into perspective

HOME REFLECTION *Journaling, Commitments and Prayer*

Personal questions ending with **Video Insights** and **T-Shirt Design!**

Don't use this as a Study Guide, but as a SCRATCH PAD!

What do you think about when you hear the word "study"? Yeah, thought so. It's bad. Well, how about when you hear the term, "Mark It Up"? Not so bad, right?

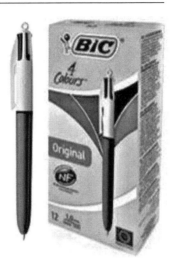

Think of a Mark-It-Up study format as the adult version of drawing with crayons.

When young children use crayons, they don't care about much except enjoying the process. That's the idea! Be like a kid. (We talked about this in Season One, Study #4.) Just swap crayons for a four-color BIC pen!

We learn through our five senses, like hearing something read aloud. So, plan on having someone who reads well read the passages.

In marking up the Scripture passage, we also use another sense that we would otherwise not, the *sense of touch*. And if we do so colorfully enter the four-color BIC pen—very inexpensive in a 12-pack from Amazon), we add just a bit more to the learning process through the *sense of sight*. (For more in-depth info on *mark it up* study: page 159.)

And don't worry about "drawing within the lines" or "color coding." Even if you tried, you just can't mess up this format. There's no right and wrong, there's just engagement. Hands on...literally.

So, think of this guide as a
SCRATCH PAD.
Apply the M-I-U format and have fun with it.
Yes, exactly like you did drawing those
childhood masterpieces!

Study and Discussion Format: WATCH > DISCOVER > RELATE

WATCH View Episode 1A Together (8:42 min.) > Discuss

Example from Study #1, Episode One:
Thunder

On next page

DISCOVER Read Text > Mark It Up > Discuss

Example from Study #1, The Word Became Flesh: John 1:1-14

Ask the "W" Questions

WHO is involved | *WHEN* did it happen | *WHERE* is it happening | *WHAT* is taking place | *HOW* is it happening... and then ask... *WHY* questions to uncover the author's original meaning.

*The *"Look For"* at the end of each **INTRO** provides initial direction.

Mark Up the passage(s) by using a four-colored BIC pen to draw:

–Shapes around (people) or /places\
–|Boxes| around whatever you'd like.
–Lines under key words and phrases.
–Clouds wherever you'd feel like it.
–Identify change of scene, watch for contrast, repetition, key words.
–Write notes On next page

RELATE How It Applies to God / Life / You > Discuss

Express Your Thoughts:
Write / discuss / live out applications from the passages in your life— your relationship with God, with others, your values, priorities, goals.

How to `WATCH` The Chosen

Look up <u>thechosen.tv</u> under the "Watch" tab. For the app go to <u>thechosen.tv/app</u> or search *The Chosen* in your Apple or Android app store. From the app, you can stream to your TV. You can find *The Chosen* on providers like Amazon Prime too.

The Chosen

Always **turn on** the **TV's closed captions** to better follow the narrative. **Darken** **the room** to better follow the action. A big TV also helps!

Note: We identify the length of each episode (from 37 to 56 minutes, excluding credits) in the WATCH sections to help you pace the study. Better to leave things unsaid than to bog down.

How to `DISCOVER` a passage's meaning: Example

Similar to Genesis   *The Word predates Time as God*

John 1: In the beginning was the Word, and the Word was with God, and the Word was God. [2] He was in the beginning with God. [3] All things were made through him, and without him was not any thing made that was made. [4] In him was life, and the life was the light of men. [5] The light shines in the darkness, and the darkness has not overcome it. [6] There was a man sent from God, whose name was John. [7] He came as a witness, to bear witness about the light, that all might believe through him. [8] He was not the light but came to bear witness about the light. [9] The true light, which gives light to everyone, was coming into the world. [10] He was in the world, and the world was made through him, yet not receive him. [12] But to all who did receive him, who believed in his name, he gave the right to become children of God....

"A man" came as a witness to "the Word," "the Light"

Light to show the world

The results of believing and receiving = becoming

How to use the guide's questions

Unlike most Bible studies, these studies take into account the fact that your group has just spent time studying (*Discover*). So, instead of using the guide's specific questions first, **start with "general questions,"** like:

> *... Set the scene, who's involved, and what are they doing?*
>
> *... What did you see (observe/notice/appreciate) in this section?*
>
> *... What strikes you (surprises you/is something new to you) here?*
>
> **Then, ask general follow-up questions like: ... Any other thoughts?**

Such questions often lead to an extended back-and-forth dialogue (see page 150). That's your discussion goal. If this happens, **you do not need to use many or any of the guide's more specific questions.** So, if/when the dialogue wanes or wanders from the main points, then you can use some of the guide's **more "specific questions,"** such as:

What are the characteristics of "The Word" in John 1?

How do Jesus' values differ from those of James and John?

Home Reflection

The end of each study provides an occasion to meditate, journal and pray over important insights. We suggest that you find a special place and a special time to schedule this as a "God-encounter thing."

Such a time allows you to express praise, embrace gratitude, plan kindnesses, and evaluate where you are giving your time, energy, and focus: *Is this what God has for you—or is there something different?*

Note the wide variety of video resources here based on themes coming out of *The Chosen*. You can more easily and directly access these videos at thechosenstudy.org, under *Guides & Extras—Season Two*.

Summarize each study in a T-Shirt Design!

The Chosen is big on merch—and so are we, except ours is drawn with a four-color BIC pen on a paper image. So, boil down your study's slogan or pick your favorite line from the episode—that's for the left-brained among us. For the right-brained, call on the artist inside to draw your idea. And, yes, share it with your group!

One more idea for your home reflection

The Chosen: 40 Days with Jesus. *The Chosen* produces devotionals for each season. They are quite good. (See page 158 for more info.)

Longer options for Study #10 (See also page 118.)

Why should you consider a longer gathering for your last meeting?

and

Why bring up the last gathering even before you've had your first one?

Good questions. The answer requires a *big picture explanation*, so here goes: *The Chosen Study* is not meant to be a "normal Bible Study group." There certainly is nothing wrong with such studies. They're great, but they are just not what we're doing here. (For more, see pages 143-144.)

Our purpose centers around inviting everyone we know to join us for a study of Jesus and his message. In doing so, we seek to build enduring friendships between us, and that's how adding a day-long or weekend bonding event (at a special place!) can help us reach these goals.

Hopefully, your last gathering won't be your last meeting, but a key bonding opportunity to add fuel to the fire of momentum... for your next Chosen Study and the new group members who will join you!

For more input on how to create such longer events, see *Leaders* at thechosenstudy.org. On the next page are two basic options:

OPTION ONE: Day-Long Study #10 Event

9:00 Breakfast	**1:30** Review: Studies #1-5/Video clips
9:30 Study #10, pp. 118-132	**3:00** Review: Studies #6-10/Video clips
12:00 Lunch	**5:00** Dinner

OPTION TWO: Weekend Study #10 Retreat

FRIDAY: Dinner	**1:30** Afternoon session
7:00 Study #10, pp. 118-132	**6:00** Saturday Dinner
SATURDAY: Breakfast	**7:30** Evening Session
9:00 Morning session	**SUNDAY:** Breakfast
12:00 Saturday Lunch	**9:00** Morning session/End with Lunch

Leader's Notes: (See also pages 143-151.)

As you look back on the format, what do you find important or helpful?

-

-

-

-

-

Leaders: For helpful video explanation of *How to Lead a Chosen Study* go here: tinyurl.com/how-to-lead and tinyurl.com/ how-to-promote.

We often use "tinyurl.com" to shorten the URL that would otherwise be required to type into your browser window to access a video.

A Word as We Begin

The Chosen is meant to take you into the eyes and ears of the people who followed Jesus. We believe that if you can see Jesus through the eyes of those who met him, you can be changed and impacted in the same way they were. If we can connect you with their burdens and struggles and questions, then ideally, we can connect you to the solution, to the answer to those questions.   –Dallas Jenkins

---

The Chosen Study supports these aspirations by pairing *The Chosen* with Old and New Testament passages to take us deeper—together!
                                                   –The Chosen Study Team

---

Starting a Chosen Study? Let us know: thechosenstudy.org/join and connect with others doing so: facebook.com/thechosenstudy. Thanks!

PRIOR to STUDY

Leading Season Two—preparation checklist

Leader's Note: *Buy guides and four-colored BIC pens in advance.* Participants can purchase guides themselves but it's often easier if one person buys the guides (from Amazon or other bookstores) along with four-color BIC pens (find 6/12 BIC pen packs on Amazon). We keep the guides affordable to encourage their widespread use. To see all our guides and to order including **volume discounts**(!), see: thechosenstudy.com/order.

Buy some extra guides for new people and those who forget to bring theirs—it will happen. **Label these as *EXTRA* on the back cover** to use for others in subsequent weeks. Feel free to charge the participants small fee for reimbursement of these purchases.

If someone forgets their guide and there are no extras, go to the website **to get the PDF by typing in URL:** thechosenstudy.org/season-two

-Study the passage(s) and take notes on the episodes ahead of time. Look at the *Notes* after the questions (and other commentaries, as you see fit), as well as the *Real But Realistic?* sections.

-Spend time preparing using Prior To Study on page 19, etc. Mark It Up! **Page 19 is the template. All other studies follow a similar pattern.**

Always tell your group at which question to end, so they know how far to go during the study/discussion time.

Keep up the pace! You often think you have more time than you do, so closely monitor time, leave things unsaid, and keep moving to end on time. (Ask your group for permission to interrupt to keep up the pace!)

NOTE TO EVERYONE: *Chosen Study* guides are not meant to be static presentations. We are open to your review, comments, and edits. If you find helpful, related videos, or commentary presentations, please let us know at thechosenstudy.org/join.

Leading Study #1—facilitating checklist

-Begin by exchanging names and personal info. Put together a sign-up sheet. (See page 152-153 and sign-up sheet on website under *Resources*.)

-Have members put their names on the back cover for identification.

-Identify your time constraints and whether you will meet as a small or small/large group combination. (See pages 7 and 146.)

-Go through the Eight Ground Rules on page 147. Talk about signing the Page 147 Pledge of consistent attendance. We're not here to lay on guilt, but consistency serves everyone. Have fun with stressing this!

-Skim/review/discuss pages 20-21. Then watch/discuss the last 12:15 minutes of episode 8 (I Am He). Then watch/discuss the Bible Project video and watch/discuss 8:18 minutes of episode 1 (Thunder).

-Discuss the study format by going through pages 8 to 16, so that everyone has a feel for the M-I-U format. At the end of all DISCOVER INTROs is a clue of what to "Look For" in the upcoming passage.

-Have a prepped volunteer summarize or read aloud the Intro and the "Look For." Read Genesis 1:1-5 and John 1:1-14 on pages 25-26.

-Give members some time for personal study using BIC pens. Monitor group(s) to end study time when appropriate. **Keep up the pace!**

-Discuss the passage by first asking general discussion questions. Then, if needed, the specific guide questions (see explanation on page 12). First discuss in small group(s) and then, if available, the large group.

-Spend time in reflection/writing and discuss the Relate questions. Point out the Home Reflection, Video Insights and T-Shirt sections (page 31-33). For links to the videos, see thechosenstudy/season-two.

Notes: What are the important things for you to focus on?

-

-

-

-

-

-

-

-

-

-

-

-

I Am He / Thunder

Study #1

FROM The CHOSEN

BACKGROUND: In Season One's guide, we detailed some history on how *The Chosen* came to be. Suffice to say, creator, Dallas Jenkins, and distributor, Angel Studios, hit a crowdfunding home run, financing Season One to the tune of 10 million dollars from a pilot episode.

Enthusiastically embraced, Season One provided the crowdfunding capital to produce Season Two, and to laid the groundwork for seven seasons in total. The series is free and funded by people interested in "paying it forward." Now it's time to watch it, study it, discuss it, and live it forward!

START WITH A REVIEW:

Take a few minutes to individually skim the events and characters in Season One on pages 22-23; then discuss it together using the questions on page 24. If you haven't seen the first season yet, no problem. Hang in there and mentally file away what you hear. Catch up as you'd like by binge-watching the first season at home (see top of page 13).

Looking Back on Season One > Discuss

Pilot Episode: The series opens with Jesus' birth story as experienced by **shepherds,** one of whom was lame. Having heard of Old Testament pro-

phecies and having seen angels, they visit **Mary, Joseph,** and **baby Jesus.** Beholding the scene, they are transformed, even healed. They tell others, in Bethlehem, and beyond, of the angels' proclamation—*the good news of great joy that will be for all the people* (Luke 2:10).

Episode One: The opening scene depicts a woman ("Lilith") in distress and demon-possessed. **Nicodemus,** a Pharisee from Jerusalem, is compelled by the Romans to exorcise her demons, but fails, causing him to question his faith. After a near-suicide attempt, Lilith meets Jesus, who calls her by her real name, **Mary of Magdala.** We also meet brothers **Simon** and **Andrew,** fishermen with tax debts, and their tax collector **Matthew,** all of whose lives are about to change.

Episode Two: To the distress of his overseer, **Gaius,** an earnest Matthew seeks out Roman praetor, **Quintus,** for help. Quintus ends up enlisting his help to catch fishermen who evade taxes on Shabbat (Sabbath). Nicodemus tracks down Mary to clarify the source of her demonic deliverance. Preparation for the Shabbat meal is made and celebrated by Jewish leaders, fishermen, Matthew with his dog, and Mary Magdalene. Mary hosts a meal for a small group, with the last arrival introduced as "the man who helped me."

Episode Three: Aptly titled, *Jesus Loves the Little Children,* the children are commended as examples for Jesus' students. All such students should listen to him and tell others about him. Through the eyes of **Abigail, Joshua "the Brave,"** and the other children, we see how kind and purposeful Jesus is. Our challenge: Embrace such a childlike faith!

Episode Four: The series pivots from Jesus with children to a defining moment in his childhood when he spent three days at the temple unbeknownst to his parents. When they found him, Jesus asks, *"Didn't you know I must be in my Father's House?"* Twenty years later, Jesus and his students attend a wedding at Cana. While there, he confound everyone—the wedding party, wine stewards, **Ramah** and **Thomas**, as well as his students—by turning water into wine. This miracle remedies the crisis at hand. This "sign" also answers his mother's challenge, *"If not now, when?"* Jesus' intervention reveals more of who he is and what he is about. Later, Nicodemus questions **John the Baptist** in prison, eager to learn more about the coming Messiah.

Episode Five: The fishermen have failed in their efforts to pay back taxes to Rome. Roman officials are not to be trifled with and Simon faces the imminent consequence of imprisonment or worse. Only a miracle can save him and that, surprisingly, is what happens. The huge catch leads Simon to repentance and faith. Jesus promises to turn fishermen into fishers of people. Simon then communicates his new vocation to his wife, Eden. She enthusiastically supports this change, telling him: *Someone finally sees in you what I have always seen. You're more than a fisherman.*

Episode Six: Jesus' compassion is on full display. He heals a leper and a paralytic, showcasing the faith of their friends. As Jesus' followers witness his care, their faith in him grows, as does the resistance among religious leaders who consider his claims and actions blasphemous. Some are jealous, while others are intrigued, as they sort out what to make of this itinerant miracle worker from Nazareth.

Episode Seven: Building common ground with Nicodemus, Jesus takes us back to Moses and the bronze serpent, which was lifted up in the wilderness, and healed God's people by faith. He calls unlikely converts to *follow me*. Matthew is called and follows immediately—much to the consternation of Simon. Jesus' disciples are divided by personal, political, and even ethnic points of views. Jesus urges Simon (and us) to: *Get used to different!*

Episode Eight: The final episode begins with a flashback to Jacob's Well. This sets up the following scene where Jesus and his students head straight through the hated and dangerous region of Samaria. Jesus stops at Jacob's Well where he meets **Photina**, an outcast woman of Samaria. Their encounter redefines the life and mission of Jesus and his disciples, as we will soon see in Season Two.

1. *Who were your three favorite characters in Season One?*

> *... How is he or she starting to be changed by getting to know Jesus as the Messiah?*

    –

    –

    –

Okay, one more: –

WATCH **View the last 10:15 min. from Season One, Episode 8** *(from 42:25 to 52.40)* **> Discuss**

INTRO: Season One ends with Jesus' encounter with a Samaritan woman (named **Photina**) at Jacob's Well in Sychar. Other women are disgusted by her lifestyle choices. So, to avoid them, Photina chooses to go to the well in the middle of the day's heat when they won't be there. That's the very time Jesus arrives.

Jesus' disciples were surprised that he even wanted to travel through Samaria. Samaritans were despised by the Jews (and vice versa). They were considered half-breed, religious inferiors. But Jesus is on a mission to reveal his identity to the town's most outcast person, to lay the groundwork for the townspeople coming to know him as the Messiah/Shepherd, searching for lost sheep in Season Two.

2. *What is it that opens up Photina's eyes to who Jesus is?*

3. She had heard the Messiah would come and now knows the Messiah personally. *What difference does this make to her?*

WATCH View *BibleProject.com, The Messiah (5 min.) > Discuss* (tinyurl.com/bible-project-messiah)

4. *From the video, how would you describe the nature and role of the Messiah?*

Thunder

Study #1 Continued

INTRO to Season Two, Episode 1 (8:18 minutes)

INTRO: In the opening scene, ten-plus years after Jesus' death, the disciples gather to mourn "Big" James' death (44 AD; Acts 12:2). **John,** the Gospel writer, interviews **Simon Peter, Andrew, Thomas,**  **Matthew, Mary Magdalene, "Little" James, Thaddeus, Nathanael** and Jesus' mother, **Mary,** who John now addresses as mother (given Jesus' instructions in John 19:26-27). They all recount their first encounters.

WATCH View Season Two, Episode 1: 1:30-9:48 min. > Discuss

5. *What struck you about John's interview with Mary, the disciples, and Mary Magdalene?*

DISCOVER Read Aloud > Mark It Up > Discuss

INTRO: God spoke, and the universe came into existence. John links the Creator's work with that of the "divine Word" (*Logos*). By referring to Jesus  as "The Word," John states that the Redeemer was present at the time of Creation, is equal to God, and a co-partner in the ongoing fulfillment of the Divine Plan. As the sun lit up the planets eons ago, so the Son of God brings light to the earth and its inhabitants now. ***Remember to ask the "W" questions (see page 12). Especially look for God's actions in Genesis and metaphors and images in John.***

The Creation of the World

GENESIS 1 In the beginning, God created the heavens and the earth. [2] The earth was without form and void, and darkness was over the face of the deep. And the Spirit of God was hovering over the face of the waters.

[3] And God said, "Let there be light," and there was light. [4] And God saw that the light was good. And God separated the light from the darkness. [5] God called the light Day, and the darkness he called Night. And there was evening and there was morning, the first day....

The Word Became Flesh

JOHN 1 In the beginning was the Word, and the Word was with God, and the Word was God. [2] He was in the beginning with God. [3] All things were made through him, and without him was not anything made that was made. [4] In him was life, and the life was the light of men. [5] The light shines in the darkness, and the darkness has not overcome it.

[6] There was a man sent from God, whose name was John. [7] He came as a witness, to bear witness about the light, that all might believe through him. [8] He was not the light but came to bear witness about the light.

[9] The true light, which gives light to everyone, was coming into the world. [10] He was in the world, and the world was made through him, yet the world did not know him. [11] He came to his own, and his own people did not receive him. [12] But to all who did receive him, who believed in his name, he gave the right to become children of God,

¹³ who were born, not of blood nor of the will of the flesh nor of the wil

of man, but of God.

¹⁴ And the Word became flesh and dwelt among us, and we have seer

his glory, glory as of the only Son from the Father, full of grace and truth

6. *How does the beginning of John's Gospel compare to the beginning*
of Genesis?

7. *What are the characteristics of "The Word" in John 1?*

8. *What does John tell us about "The Word's" reception, both positively*
and negatively, in the world?

RELATE *How It Applies to God / Life / You > Discuss*

9. Imagine that John had interviewed you while writing his gospel. *How would you describe how and when you first encountered Jesus?*

NOTES on Study #1 *Commentary and Historical Context*

John 4:1-39—Having our Thirst Quenched and Hunger Satisfied

- *The Chosen* identifies Photina as an outcast in her hometown. She visited the well when other women didn't, has had "five husbands," and experienced a great deal of shame and rejection. Jesus offers her *living water* to meet her deepest need—a relationship with himself.

- As *living water* replenishes the spirit, so *living food*—doing God's will—sustains the soul. The disciples miss the point in their asking if Jesus had already eaten. But, not to worry, next stop is Sychar, where Photina is now preparing the way for their arrival!

Genesis 1:1-5 & John 1:1-14—The Creation of the World/The Word

- Be sure to notice that the first three words in both Genesis and The Gospel of John are "In the beginning." Genesis tells us that *time* was the first thing created, but in John's Gospel, "The Word," Jesus, preceded even *time*. "The Word," brought us God's light, so we could see and experience his grace and truth (v. 14).

- The word, translated as "overcome" in John 1:5, has a double meaning. An alternate translation is "comprehended" or "apprehended." It indicates both that humans have failed to understand the Light, and that darkness has been unable to extinguish it.

That's plausible but did it happen?

Was the Samaritan woman named Photina? We don't know. However, outside of Jesus' inner circle, she is the first to whom he reveals his identity as the Messiah. Likewise, it was to women that Jesus first appeared after the Resurrection. Such historical details were initially detrimental to the validation of his identity, since women had no societal status as witnesses in a court of law. However, they are now a powerful testimony of the New Testament's authenticity, because no ancient writer would have made up a story with women witnesses!

John 4 contains Jesus' longest conversation on record. His engagement with the Samaritan woman turned her shame to zeal for the one "who told me everything I've ever done." She now becomes the town crier for her hometown of Sychar, which is exactly where Jesus and his disciples are headed to spend the next two days.

Eastern Orthodox tradition contends that the name given her at baptism was Photini—meaning, "enlightened one." Stories about her became embellished, but likely contain kernels of truth. Some asserted that she was "equal to the apostles" for her zeal. After Jesus' resurrection, some traditions have her speaking about Jesus throughout Asia Minor. Others suggest she went to Rome where, under Nero, she was eventually martyred along with her two sons.

Did all the disciples meet to be interviewed by John for his Gospel? We have no record from whom, where, or when the Gospel writers collected their stories. There is a fact-finding reference in Luke 1:1-4. Luke said he investigated eyewitness accounts in documenting Jesus stories and sayings, to keep them for posterity.

The Chosen envisions the disciples meeting and mourning the death of "Big" James. He died at the hands of Herod the Great's grandson Herod Agrippa I (reigned 41-44 AD). Acts 12 records Herod's violence toward early church leaders in Jerusalem: *He killed James, the brother of John, with the sword* (Acts 12:2).

HOME REFLECTION *Journaling, Commitments and Prayer*

10. *What things about Jesus have you learned since you first met him?*

11. *What difference did Jesus make in the lives of his followers?*

... What difference has he made (or would you like him to make) in your life?

The Chosen: **40 Days with Jesus.** *The Chosen* produces a devotional for each season which can be used five days a week over the course of this study. We highly recommend it. (See page 158 for more info.)

Video Insight: John 1, Creation Series —The Bible Project
Type in URL: tinyurl.com/bible-project-john1 (6:30 min.)
(Type URL precisely in your browser on device or go to website under *Guides*.

Notes: **Other Videos:**

After watching > discovering > relating,
what slogan would you write or draw on your T-shirt?

Draft concepts:

Final design:

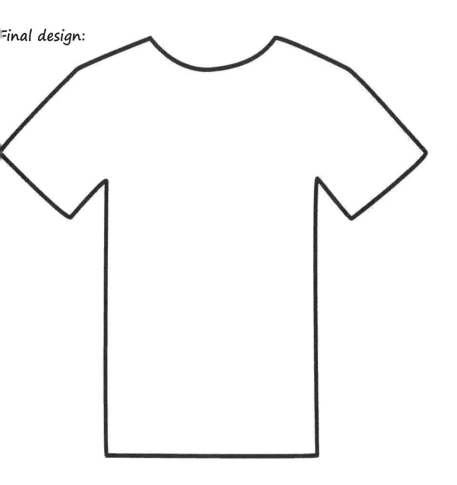

 Getting ready for the next study

—Begin with new people introducing themselves and again point out the ground rules on page 147

—Briefly reacquaint your group with the study format on pages 12-1 especially the "W" questions and using the BIC pens. At the end of eac of the DISCOVER INTROs is a clue of **what to "Look For"** in the passage

NOTE TO EVERYONE: *HOME REFLECTION. The Chosen Study* is no written with the expectation that participants do prior preparation However, we do encourage a post-study time of reflection (like on pages 29-31 and 39-41): to journal, consider life-commitments, and to pray.

So, schedule time, maybe as part of a weekly Sabbath (see Season One Study 2) to go deeper with the content's application in your life. Oh and do feel free to look/study ahead of time if you'd like!

You've also likely noted a suggested video for *further insight* (pages 32 42, etc.). These videos are meant to introduce you to those who are speaking about *The Chosen* or on its themes and take you deeper into the content. To access, it is necessary to **precisely type the URL** in you computer, device or phone's browser window.

You can also access these videos at our website, thechosenstudy.org under *Guides & Extras—Season Two.*

Thunder

INTRO: Many Samaritans were open to Jesus, as were those in Sychar (John 4:39-42). But some could not get over their racial prejudices against the Jews. One Samaritan village—not Sychar, but the unnamed one cited in Luke 9:51-55—is a case in point. Noticing Jesus heading through their village to Jerusalem, they did not provide provisions for him, nor did they invite him to stay with them. This was an act of extreme, even spiteful, inhospitality.

Look for the action/reactions of the characters in the stories.

DISCOVER Read Aloud > Mark It Up > Discuss

JOHN 4 [39] Many Samaritans from that town [Sychar] believed in him because of the woman's testimony, "He told me all that I ever did." [40] So when the Samaritans came to him, they asked him to stay with them, and he stayed there two days. [41] And many more believed because of his word.

[42] They said to the woman, "It is no longer because of what you said that we believe, for we have heard for ourselves, and we know that this is indeed the Savior of the world."

A Samaritan Village Rejects Jesus

LUKE 9 [51] When the days drew near for him to be taken up, he set his face to go to Jerusalem. [52] And he sent messengers ahead of him, who went and entered a village of the Samaritans, to make preparations for him. [53] But the people did not receive him, because his face was set toward Jerusalem. [54] And when his disciples James and John saw it, they said, "Lord, do you want us to tell fire to come down from heaven and consume them?" [55] But he turned and rebuked them. [56] And they went on to another village.

1. *What is similar and what is different in these two stories?*

2. *How do Jesus' values differ from those of James and John?*

WATCH *View Episode 1B starting at 10:45 (53 min.)* > **Discuss**

INTRO: In Sychar of Samaria, James and John are to till a field owned by **Melech,** a man crippled by an accident and living with shame, which are the result of a past crime. Melech, with his wife,  Chedva, and daughter, **Rebecca,** host Jesus and his band of followers for dinner. Their meal is one which the disciples bought earlier that day.

Later that night, back in Sychar, Jesus and his band meet up again with Photina and her now reconciled husband, **Neriah.** They open their home to them for a night's rest.

We also meet **Kafni,** the vineyard owner, who appreciates Jesus' "action" which saved his business' reputation. However, he is concerned about protecting his daughter, Ramah, from the risks of joining Jesus, Thomas, and the others.

3. The Ramah-Kafni-Jesus' encounter raises issues of how faith in Jesus can bring tension between family members. *How was this tension handled differently:*

   … by Ramah?

   … by Kafni?

   … by Jesus?

4. The disciples worry that Jesus is lost when, in fact, he is seeking the lost. *In what ways does Jesus seek out people in this episode?*

DISCOVER *Read Aloud > Mark It Up > Discuss*

INTRO: Nobody likes to lose things, including God. As the Good Shepherd, Jesus seeks and finds the sheep that stray, joyfully welcoming them home to live under his protection and care. Sadly, the  religious leaders of his day did not share these same values, but neither, by and large, did his disciples. Yet, for those who come to him with humility and repentance, it all starts to make sense. ***Focus on the shepherd's action and the emotions describe in this passage.***

The Parable of the Lost Sheep

LUKE 15 Now the tax collectors and sinners were all drawing near to hear him. ² And the Pharisees and the scribes grumbled, saying, "This man receives sinners and eats with them."

³ So he told them this parable: ⁴ "What man of you, having a hundred sheep, if he has lost one of them, does not leave the ninety-nine in the open country, and go after the one that is lost, until he finds it? ⁵ And when he has found it, he lays it on his shoulders, rejoicing. ⁶ And when he comes home, he calls together his friends and his neighbors, saying to them, 'Rejoice with me, for I have found my sheep that was lost.' ⁷ Just so, I tell you, there will be more joy in heaven over one sinner who repents than over ninety-nine righteous persons who need no repentance.

5. *Compare Jesus' values with those of the Jewish religious leaders?*

5. How do you feel when you find something that has been lost? Give an example?

... What does this teach you about heaven's reaction to finding lost people?

RELATE How It Applies to God / Life / You > Discuss

7. Do you consider yourself "found" by Jesus, or, in some ways, is he still "looking for you"? Describe.

8. What does it (or could it) mean to you to be "found" by him?

NOTES on Study #2 *Commentary and Historical Context*

Luke 9:51-56—Samaritan Opposition

- James and John's request to bring down fire alludes to the story of Elijah calling down fire on the soldiers of Ahaziah. This Samaritan ruler twice tried to have Elijah seized, each time with no success but with significant loss of life (2 Kings 1:9-12).

   Jesus, however, had given very specific instructions about how to appropriately respond to those who refused to receive him. Calling down fire wasn't part of the equation! When rejected, the disciples were to shake dust from their feet as a testimony against the city and move on (Luke 9:5; 10:10-12).

   Jesus taught about God's judgment toward those who reject him (Luke 10:12-14; 13:1-9). But God is merciful (Psalm 85:15; 103:8, 145:8). The disciples are to leave any such judgment in God's hands.

Luke 15:1-7—The Parable of the Lost Sheep

- Tax collectors, like Matthew, worked for the Roman occupation and were considered traitors to their nation. They were lumped in with other "lowlife sinners," despised and shunned by fellow Jews.

- The grumbling of the Pharisees and scribes stood in stark contrast to the rejoicing in heaven over "one sinner" who repents.

That's plausible but did it happen?

Was Jesus criticized for "hanging out" with the wrong kind of people? Yes. To the Pharisees it was scandalous that Jesus would associate with tax collectors, sinners, and others of ill repute. But Jesus insisted that he had "come to seek and to save the lost." (Luke 19:10)

Figuring out the motivations of the Pharisees and other Jewish leaders can be challenging. Some are zealous and envious of Jesus' abilities and influence. Others were judgmental and stuck on their own flawed interpretation of the Old Testament law. Still others worried for the threat he posed to their power and sway over the people. Many ended up believing and following Jesus, but not until after his resurrection.

How does this Samaritan landowner, Melech, fit the biblical story?
The character of Melech is unique to the film and not mentioned in the Gospels. *The Chosen* producers use Melech as a means of introducing the Parable of the Good Samaritan (Luke 10:25-37), in which a traveling Jew is beaten and robbed. This left-for-dead Jew is rescued by a "Good" Samaritan, one who stops to help, and pays for his convalescence.

The "Good Samaritan" in Jesus' parable contrasts sharply with Melech, the "Bad Samaritan." In the film, Melech becomes lame when thrown from the horse he stole from a Jew he robbed. Even though the Bible says nothing about such circumstances, the spiritual and emotional healing he receives is typical of the mercy Jesus displayed to people like him. It becomes a point of teaching for the disciples, who would have a hard time ever envisioning a Samaritan being the good guy. (Note "Big" James' and John's nonverbals as Melech tells his story!)

Melech's character further provides the connection to Jesus' parable about a lost sheep toward the beginning of the episode. Melech is the lost sheep for whom the owner will search, despite having ninety-nine other sheep that are safe (Matthew 18:12-14). He leaves them to find the one that is lost and rejoices when the lost is found.

HOME REFLECTION *Journaling, Commitments and Prayer*

9. On the following continuum, put an "X" on the line in the place that best describes your relationship with God/Jesus right now.

Observer...   Skeptic...   Learner...   Seeker...   Follower...

10. Do you want to move further to the right on the spectrum? If so, what might that mean for you?

11. *Who could help, and what could you do to encourage such growth?*

Video Insight: The Lost Sheep –Trent Vineyard
Type in URL: <u>tinyurl.com/the-lost-sheep</u> (5:40 min.)

Notes: **Other Videos:**

After watching > discovering > relating,
what slogan would you write or draw on your T-shirt?

Draft concepts:

Final design:

 *Periodically remind your group of two things*

NOTE TO EVERYONE: *HOME REFLECTION.* As your group members if they have been using these questions, and if there is anything that they would like to share (pages 29, 39 and, the next one, on page 49) Such "at home time" also gives group members time to read through the *Notes* and the *Real But Realistic?* sections.

-Keep inviting new people. One advantage of *The Chosen Study* is that new members can come in at any time and binge watch to catch up.

Who to invite? Anyone who fits on this list: friends, family members, colleagues, teammates, acquaintances, those who cross your path—if they're curious, if they're willing to check it out—then come!

I Saw You

INTRO: We may be on top of the mountain and, with a turn of circumstances, find ourselves in the valley. Depression, despair, disappointment with life and with God overwhelm us as life turns nasty.

Valley experiences are painful. They can make us "forget" about God's unrelenting love for us, as we suffer from the effects of the evils, principalities, and powers of this world.

What follows are the words of a man who felt free to honestly cry out to God concerning his deep sense of despair and abandonment. This short psalm from David's life will help prepare us for the upcoming episode of *The Chosen*.

Use your pen to underline (box-in or circle) David's list of complaints and affirmations.

How Long, O Lord? To the choirmaster. A Psalm of David.

Psalm 13 How long, O LORD? Will you forget me forever?

How long will you hide your face from me?

² How long must I take counsel in my soul

and have sorrow in my heart all the day?

How long shall my enemy be exalted over me?

³ Consider and answer me, O LORD my God;

light up my eyes, lest I sleep the sleep of death,

⁴ lest my enemy say, "I have prevailed over him,"

lest my foes rejoice because I am shaken.

⁵ But I have trusted in your steadfast love;

my heart shall rejoice in your salvation.

⁶ I will sing to the LORD,

because he has dealt bountifully with me.

1. David feels free to honestly state his pain to God. *How does he describe the extent of his desperation?*

2. *What gives David hope in the midst of his painful struggle?*

WATCH   **View Episode 2** (50 min., from 0:00 to 52:22) > **Discuss**

INTRO: In this episode, the disciples welcome **Philip,** a follower of John the Baptist and a friend of Andrew. Upon encountering Jesus as the Messiah, he seeks out an old friend, **Nathanael,**

with whom he shares the Good News. Nathanael (a failed architect by the show's script) was despondent over the loss of a collapsed building and his career. His perspective changes after meeting the man who saw him under a fig tree and answered his prayer.

3. *Beyond losing his job, what has brought Nathanael to this low point?*

4. Nathanael quotes from a similar psalm of lament and wonders aloud, "Do you see me?" *How would you describe his pain?*

DISCOVER   **Read Aloud > Mark It Up > Discuss**

INTRO: Nathanael is stunned that Jesus knows and deeply understands him, even before their meeting in person. Jesus answers this seeker's prayer meant for God alone. And it has the

desire effect of gaining another follower who came and saw. ***Identify the series of questions and answers.***

Jesus Calls Philip and Nathanael

JOHN 1 [43] The next day Jesus decided to go to Galilee. He found Philip and said to him, "Follow me."

44 Now Philip was from Bethsaida, the city of Andrew and Peter. 45 Philip found Nathanael and said to him, "We have found him of whom Moses in the Law and also the prophets wrote, Jesus of Nazareth, the son of Joseph."

46 Nathanael said to him, "Can anything good come out of Nazareth?" Philip said to him, "Come and see."

47 Jesus saw Nathanael coming toward him and said of him, "Behold, an Israelite indeed, in whom there is no deceit!

48 Nathanael said to him, "How do you know me?" Jesus answered him, "Before Philip called you, when you were under the fig tree, I saw you."

49 Nathanael answered him, "Rabbi, you are the Son of God! You are the King of Israel!"

50 Jesus answered him, "Because I said to you, 'I saw you under the fig tree,' do you believe? You will see greater things than these." 51 And he said to him, "Truly, truly, I say to you, you will see heaven opened and the angels of God ascending and descending on the Son of Man."

5. *Describe this scene and the invitations made in it.*

6. *What effect does "being seen" by Jesus have on Nathanael?*

RELATE How It Applies to God / Life / You > Discuss

7. When have you felt unseen by others in your life?

... What would it have meant in that circumstance to know that God himself "sees you"?

NOTES on Study #3 Commentary and Historical Context

Psalm 13:1-6—How Long, O Lord?

- This psalm of lament depicts a low point in David's life and is used here to capture Nathanael's likely mood. When we sense our prayers are not getting through, we feel forgotten, even unloved. This is not a time to "hold back" our feelings. God is not intimidated. He wants his wisdom and kindness to bring hope to our despair.

John 1:43-51—Jesus Calls Philip and Nathanael

- The "Prophet to come," anticipated by John the Baptist and Philip (John 1:21,45), is the one Moses wrote about. However great Moses was, this one was like him, only greater (Deuteronomy 18:18).

- The "greater things" that the disciples will see likely alludes to the miracles Jesus (and his disciples) will perform, including the greatest one—the resurrection.

- The "Son of Man" here, as elsewhere, is a title that Jesus takes on, conveying divine authority (see Daniel 7:13-14).

 **That's plausible but did it happen?**

Was Nathanael an architect whose building collapsed? We have no record of this. But his despair over such a personal and career setback feels realistic enough to send one "over the edge." Time spent seeking solace from God made him open to the invitation to follow Jesus. This invitation was first extended by Philip, and then by Jesus himself.

Did Matthew, the learned tax collector, become a woodsman?
We don't know what the disciples did in camp. Undoubtedly, they had much to learn, not only from Jesus, but also from each other. As they "delighted" in provoking Matthew, so we delight in seeing his character develop. And, of course, you can expect, the tables will turn!

Did Peter take Jesus aside to lecture him on organizing the mission?
The disciples likely struggled to follow an itinerant teacher whose day-to-day schedule seemed haphazard. Peter opposed Jesus' willingness to suffer and die (Matthew 16:21-28), and we also know he became a leader in the early Church (Acts 2–12). Such traits surfaced early on and were commended by Jesus, in due time (Matthew 16:13-18).

The women want to study Torah and the Prophets, so how did they?
Girls were denied the Hebrew school offered to boys. But, as the series points out, it matters little how much you know if you don't know the Messiah. It was possible, even likely, that girls and women learned from the men in their lives, as portrayed in *The Chosen*, where Mary Magdalene learns Scripture and how to read from her father.

If school or Scripture memory made all the difference, the Pharisees would have been Jesus' favorites. Instead, he equips the unlearned with the experience of a lifetime, by allowing them to directly learn his character and his ways. Such an opportunity naturally encourages many to dig deeper into the truths of what he taught.

NOTE TO EVERYONE: Our hope in these Studies is to foster the kind of commitment to be *Scripture learners* exhibited by these disciples!

<u>**HOME REFLECTION**   *Journaling, Commitments and Prayer*</u>

8. When did you first sense the call to *"come and see"*?

9. What has especially opened you up to seeing God at work in you?

    a)   A painful loss or setback—at work or with family...
    b)   The Psalms—or other beautiful, good, and true poetry...
    c)   Anything that reminds you of "home"—where the heart is...
    d)   Journaling—letting the emotions flow without editing...
    e)   Other...
       Explain:

10. What of God's character and work have you seen in your life recently?

Video Insight: Psalm 139: A Journey into Identity -Scott Harper

Type in URL: <u>tinyurl.com/psalm-139</u> (13:56 min.)

Notes: *Other Videos:*

After watching > discovering > relating,
what slogan would you write or draw on your T-shirt?

Draft concepts:

Final design:

 ## Some reminders

Remember, always tell your group at which question to end, so they know how far to go during the study/discussion time.

Keep up the pace! You often think you have more time than you do so, closely monitor your time, leave things unsaid, and keep moving to end on time.

NOTE FOR EVERYONE: *Inviting new people—is it too late?* No way! The beauty of *The Chosen Study* is that new members can come in at any time and binge watch to catch up! Additionally, we've seen people go through each Season multiple times.

Matthew 4:24

Study #4

FROM
The BIBLE

INTRO: There are 37 specific references to Jesus' miracles in the Gospels, of which Matthew 4:24 is one. Jesus' resurrection and other general descriptions of divine intervention add to this number. Of course, there may well have been hundreds, if not thousands, of miracles which went unrecorded.

Matthew (in film and Scripture) captures Jesus ministering to great crowds, day after day, with lines of people coming to him for healing. We can imagine the disciples wondered, even debated, what kind of Messiah would serve such great crowds. He does so as a humble healer, not as the great warrior they had envisioned before meeting.

Look for the words that describe the people who came to Jesus and where they came from (also see map on pages 138-139).

DISCOVER *Read Aloud > Mark It Up > Discuss*

Jesus Ministers to Great Crowds

Matthew 4 [23] And he went throughout all Galilee, teaching in their synagogues and proclaiming the gospel of the kingdom and healing every disease and every affliction among the people. [24] So his fame spread throughout all Syria, and they brought him all the sick, those afflicted with various diseases and pains, those oppressed by demons, those having seizures, and paralytics, and he healed them. [25] And great crowds followed him from Galilee and the Decapolis, and from Jerusalem and Judea, and from beyond the Jordan.

1. Identify and locate the cities and villages named above, on the map on pages 138-139. This passage tells us that great crowds were following Jesus. *What do you believe attracted them to him?*

WATCH *View Episode 3 (35 min., from 1:30 to 36:17) > Discuss*

INTRO: In this episode, no new characters are introduced. Instead, we get a deeper insight into Jesus' students and their continuing journey of faith. Mary (Jesus' mother) surprises all with her stories of raising Jesus from infancy—again underscoring his humanity.

Tensions erupt between disciples as they share their own background stories and resentments towards one another. This show of anger ends abruptly as they witness Jesus' exhaustion after a full day's work of healing. It's not hard to imagine ourselves in that circle.

2. *With which of the issues that the disciples discussed (politics, healing, fame, or losing a parent) can you readily identify?*

3. *How does Jesus' example speak to the bickering among the disciples?*

DISCOVER   Read Aloud > Mark It Up > Discuss

INTRO: Jesus' example to his disciples is a powerful one, both in the episode and in this passage from Paul to the Philippian believers. (See page 60 for more background.) ***Look for repeated words and contrasts.***

Christ's Example of Humility

Philippians 2 [1] So if there is any encouragement in Christ, any comfort from love, any participation in the Sprit, any affection and sympathy, [2] complete my joy by being of the same mind, having the same love, being in full accord and of one mind. [3] Do nothing from selfish ambition or conceit, but in humility count others more significant than yourselves. [4] Let each of you look not only to his own interests, but also to the interests of others. [5] Have this mind among yourselves, which is yours in Christ Jesus,

[6] who, though he was in the form of God,

did not count equality with God a thing to be grasped,

[7] but emptied himself,

by taking the form of a servant,

being born in the likeness of men.

8 And being found in human form,

he humbled himself

by becoming obedient to the point of death,

even death on a cross.

9 Therefore God has highly exalted him

and bestowed on him the name that is above every name,

10 so that at the name of Jesus every knee should bow,

in heaven and on earth and under the earth,

11 and every tongue confess that Jesus Christ is Lord,

to the glory of God the Father.

Lights in the World

12 Therefore, my beloved, as you have always obeyed, so now, not only as in my presence but much more in my absence, work out your own salvation with fear and trembling, **13** for it is God who works in you both to will and to work for his good pleasure.

14 Do all things without grumbling or disputing, **15** that you may be blameless and innocent, children of God without blemish in the midst of a crooked and twisted generation, among whom you shine as lights in the world, **16** holding fast to the word of life, so that in the day of Christ I may be proud that I did not run in vain or labor in vain. **17** Even if I am to be poured out as a drink offering upon the sacrificial offering of your faith, I am glad and rejoice with you all. **18** Likewise you also should be glad and rejoice with me.

4. The apostle Paul writes to the church at Philippi to encourage unity. *What does he say here about how we are to live with others?*

5. *How does Jesus exemplify humility for all who would follow him?*

6. *How will our relationships with each other act as a "light in the world" (v. 15)?*

RELATE How It Applies to God / Life / You > Discuss

7. *What example(s) of Christ-like living have you seen in someone close to you?*

... How has he or she influenced you?

NOTES on Study #4 *Commentary and Historical Context*

Matthew 4:23-25; Jesus Ministers to Great Crowds

• Recall the "W" question from page 8: *Where* did it happen? Find map locations (pages 138-139). The Decapolis referred to a league of ten Gentile (non-Jewish or pagan) cities situated east of the Jordan river.

Philippians 2:1-18—Christ's Example of Humility

• *The Chosen* depicts Jesus pouring himself into the lives of many and healing all who came to him. The very act of Jesus leaving heaven, and all other acts that followed, modeled the greatest humility in history in serving others. The self-sacrifice of Jesus stands in sharp contrast to the disciples and is the basis for the correction that Paul seeks to instill in the lives of the Philippian church.

Philippi was a Roman colony. The small church Paul established there was under considerable outside pressure, but he was more concerned about disunity from within. Unlike today, believers who did not get along could not simply leave and go to another church but needed to work it out. Paul points them to Jesus' model of humility, which also serves as a tremendous example for us.

• More than a model of humility, Jesus epitomizes what it means to be fully human. Paul describes the incarnational event as that of God taking on flesh, becoming man. In so doing, God in Jesus comes to be identified as one of us, a vulnerable human being. Jesus the Son leaves behind his privileges (not his deity) when he submits to the Father's will. Jesus accepts punishment for our sin—though totally innocent—as an act of pure grace, thus redeeming us from sin. Even so, Paul's teaching here in this section is not meant to describe what Christ's act means to us, so much as what it meant to Jesus himself.

• Verses 6-11 are arranged in poetic couplets. For this reason, scholars suggest that these verses may be excerpted from an early Christian confession, creed, or hymn. Whether this *Hymn to Christ* was a quote or written by Paul himself, it beautifully depicts Jesus' mission of servanthood. Paul fleshes out what Mark wrote: Jesus *"came not to be served but to serve, and to give his life as a ransom for many"* (10:45). His service fully glorifies God the Father (Philippians 2:11).

That's plausible but did it happen?

Did the disciples turn on each other, as Simon and Andrew, even Thomas, did to Matthew? We have no biblical record of such interactions, but such scuffles likely occurred given. The Pharisees often criticized Jesus for hanging out with them and other "sinners"—maybe even raising doubts among his own disciples (see Matthew 5:46, 11:19).

Was Matthew autistic?

The film characterizes Matthew as a socially awkward savant. He is depicted as a whiz kid, good with numbers, and on the autism spectrum. As such he is a target of scorn from the disciples, especially Simon. This is not an unfair character development for *The Chosen* film writers to do. This backstory is intriguing and plausible, given his occupation as a Jew working for the Romans and making money by overcharging. But we have no direct biblical evidence for him being autistic.

The potential problem stems from the powerful, visual nature of film (and the music score behind it) that can easily sweep us up and have us assigning meaning from it to the written word. We would say do both: study what the Scripture actually says and enjoy the captivating ride *The Chosen* takes us on—but learn the difference! If you'd like more input on this, check out Dallas' videos, *Can you trust The Chosen?* and the *Interview of Jonathan Roumie*, the actor who portrays Jesus. See page 140 for more info and those video links.

Did Jesus' mother and other women follow him with the Twelve?

There is no record of this, but we know Mary pondered many aspects of bringing Jesus into the world (Luke 2:19, 34-35). Like all moms, she wanted to be helpful and cared for her son in the best way she could.

We see that Mary is with Jesus at the temple (Luke 2:41-52), at the wedding in Cana (John 2:1-5), even questioned his sanity (Mark 3:21), and was present at the Cross (John 19:25-27). Mary was among the disciples at the Ascension (Acts 1:14) and could have been among the unnamed women following Jesus in his public ministry. See Luke 8:1-3 for a listing of other women who followed and ministered to Jesus.

HOME REFLECTION Journaling, Commitments and Prayer

8. How does Jesus' act of humility and sacrifice affect your priorities or perspective?

9. In what context, or with whom, is God calling you to "practice" this posture of humility?

Video Insight: Seven Things You Don't Know About Matthew
Type in URL: tinyurl.com/about-matthew –Brandon Robbins

Notes: **Other Videos:** (21:46 min.)

After watching > discovering > relating, what slogan would you write or draw on your T-shirt?

Draft concepts:

Final design:

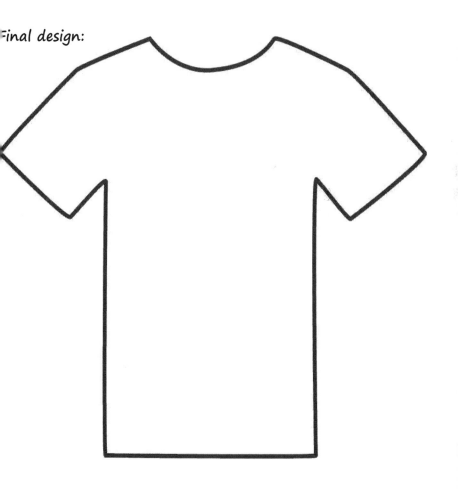

 **A reminder**

NOTE TO EVERYONE: *HOME REFLECTION.* Maybe you have not yet gotten to this section "at home." No problem. But don't miss this upcoming reflection section (on pages 71-72). The questions, honestly asked and answered, will help you deepen your relationship with God. And the *Real But Realistic?* section is nothing if not entertaining!

The Perfect Opportunity

INTRO: Jesus and his disciples head to Jerusalem to partake in the Festival of the Tabernacles (or Booths). He takes three disciples into the city where two groups plan evil—misguided Zealots, who would kill to subvert Roman rule, and a group of self-righteous Pharisees, who would trap Jesus as a false, Sabbath-breaking prophet.

In this episode, we meet **Jesse**, who is permanently lame from a childhood accident, and his brother, **Simon the Zealot**. Though conjecture, Simon is shown to have trained with a splinter group of Zealots named after the Sica dagger, called the Sicarii (literally "dagger men"), who assassinated Romans and Roman sympathizers. Considered the first terrorist sect, when a kill was made, they would scream together with bystanders to blend back into a crowd and escape detection.

WATCH | View Episode 4 (56 min., from 0:00 to 56:00) > Discuss

The events that led up to a climax at the Pool of Bethesda include:

... **child [Jesse]** falls from a tree and becomes an invalid for life.

... **Simon the Zealot** (the brother of Jesse) leaves home to become a dagger-fighting assassin, bent on killing a Roman ruler.

... **Big James** pushes ahead to celebrate the Festival of Booths.

... **Roman magistrates** gather to share intel on the assassin's plot.

... **Shmuel and other Pharisees** are on the lookout for trouble.

... **Simon, John** and **Matthew** follow Jesus to the Pool of Bethesda.

... **Jesus** performs a miracle on the Sabbath, stirring up the water!

1. *What did you learn about the Festival of Tabernacles from the discussion among the disciples and Jesus during their feast?*

... What is the significance for them and for us?

2. *What thoughts do you think Jesus may have had as he passed the condemned men being crucified at the city gate?*

3. *What do you think led a man like Simon (the Zealot) to make such an extreme commitment to violence?*

4. *In a word or phrase, what impact did Jesus' actions at the pool have:*

... on Jesse?

... on Simon the Zealot?

... on Atticus?

... on the Pharisees?

... on the three disciples?

DISCOVER Read Aloud > Mark It Up > Discuss

INTRO: This legendary Pool of Bethesda, fed by underground springs, was believed to have healing powers when the waters were stirred. Unlike *The Chosen*, John gives us no backstory, so we,  along with *The Chosen writers,* are left to speculate about the details. *Identify, with your pen, the questions and the answers.*

The Healing at the Pool on the Sabbath

JOHN 5 After this there was a feast of the Jews, and Jesus went up to Jerusalem. ² Now there is in Jerusalem by the Sheep Gate a pool, in Aramaic called Bethesda, which has five roofed colonnades. ³ In these lay a multitude of invalids—blind, lame, and paralyzed. ⁵ One man was there who had been an invalid for thirty-eight years. ⁶ When Jesus saw him lying there and knew that he had already been there a long time, he said to him, "Do you want to be healed?"

⁷ The sick man answered him, "Sir, I have no one to put me into the pool when the water is stirred up, and while I am going another steps down before me."

⁸ Jesus said to him, "Get up, take up your bed, and walk." ⁹ And at once the man was healed, and he took up his bed and walked.

Now that day was the Sabbath. [10] So the Jews said to the man who had been healed, "It is the Sabbath, and it is not lawful for you to take up your bed."

[11] But he answered them, "The man who healed me, that man said to me, 'Take up your bed, and walk.'"

[12] They asked him, "Who is the man who said to you, 'Take up your bed and walk'?"

[13] Now the man who had been healed did not know who it was, for Jesus had withdrawn, as there was a crowd in the place.

[14] Afterward Jesus found him in the temple and said to him, "See, you are well! Sin no more, that nothing worse may happen to you." [15] The man went away and told the Jews that it was Jesus who had healed him.

[16] And this was why the Jews were persecuting Jesus, because he was doing these things on the Sabbath. [17] But Jesus answered them, "My Father is working until now, and I am working."

5. *Why do you think Jesus asked the man a seemingly obvious question, "Do you want to be healed?"*

6. *What does the man's excuse reveal about him?*

7. What did Jesus want the man to learn from this miracle (5:14)?

RELATE How It Applies to God / Life / You > Discuss

8. When have you relied on excuses, instead of taking responsibility for a choice you made, for an unkind word said, or for a character flaw?

9. What would it mean for you to look to God, rather than yourself, to help you change in an area in which you struggle?

NOTES on Study #5 Commentary and Historical Context

John 5:1-17—The Healing at the Pool on the Sabbath

- The "feast of the Jews" (John 5:1) isn't specifically identified but assumed to be the *Feast of the Tabernacles* (or Booths). This week-long fall festival commemorated Israel's 40-year journey in the wilderness before entering the *Promised Land*.

- The Pool of Bethesda was discovered in the 19th century under an abandoned Byzantine church. Archaeological evidence reveals a trapezoid-shaped pool about 200 X 300 feet, divided into two pools. To make sense of its attraction as a source of healing, a later scribe added this explanation to John 5: *3b ... waiting for the moving of the water; 4 for an angel of the Lord went down at certain seasons into the pool and stirred the water: whoever stepped in first after the stirring of the water was healed of whatever disease he had.* (This scribal addition is omitted from most Bible translations.)

- By inviting the lame man to "take up your mat," Jesus gives him something to do. This returns a measure of control and dignity to the man, not to mention bids him to clean up after himself. To carry one's bedding may also be Jesus' way of repudiating the Pharisees' self imposed rules about not "working" on the Sabbath. The Law of Moses did not forbid carrying one's bedding on the Sabbath, but Jewish oral tradition did—something unimportant to Jesus.

- We aren't sure exactly why Jesus told this man to "stop sinning" (v 14). He obviously knew something about the man that we don't. One thing that appears to be true is that the healing did not relate to faith but only to the grace of God toward an undeserving man. A common belief in that day held that infirmities were the result of parental or personal sin, a belief not shared by Jesus (see John 9:1-3). Evidently no faith/healing formula prompts God's mercy either. What prompts him often remains a mystery, and we rejoice in it, as we witness the freedom of a new life.

That's plausible but did it happen?

Was Simon the Zealot the brother of the invalid man Jesse?

Not that we know of. This believable backstory dovetails two followers of Jesus, one of whom becomes a zealous apostle. But there is no biblical evidence of a brotherly connection.

Was Simon the Zealot ever close to assassinating a Roman ruler? It is possible to believe Simon trained as a fighter with the *Sicarii,* using a deadly curved dagger (see page 65). The Zealots, though not generally assassins, were an extremist political party known for covert acts of violence. They were willing to be martyrs to subvert Roman rule. One other martyr and Zealot named in Scripture was Judas, the Galilean (Acts 5:37). In this episode, Simon is bent on assassination to avenge the Jews and bring justice to the hated Romans.

What about *The Chosen's* timeline regarding the disciples?
The Chosen depicts the healing of Simon the Zealot's brother as the situation that prompted him to follow the Messiah. In their timeline, Simon had no prior encounters with Jesus but believed that the Messiah would "save the lame and gather the outcast" (Zephaniah 3:19).

The New Testament identifies a sequence of the first disciples who met and followed Jesus. The first four included Andrew, Simon, James, and John (Matthew 4:18-22; Mark 1:16-20; Luke 5:4-11). Later, Philip and Nathanael (John 1:35-51) were added. Then Matthew was called separately (Matthew 9:9-13; Mark 2:13-17 and Luke 5:27-32).

Scripture does not describe the calling of the other five disciples, nor the order in which they came. *The Chosen* suggests a possible order and circumstances. But the Gospel writers simply list or recap "the Twelve" as the ones Jesus chose. That there were *twelve* was important, because it hearkens back to the original twelve tribes of Israel, now with "new leadership," under Jesus as the promised Messiah.

HOME REFLECTION *Journaling, Commitments and Prayer*

---

10. Imagine Jesus challenging you, "Do you want to be healed?" *To what might he be referring in your life?*

... How long has this "malady" been going on?

... What would be your response? ... or excuse?

11. *What would it mean to trust God through Jesus more fully, rathe. than relying on our own resources and making excuses?*

Video Insight: The Chosen, Pool of Bethesda scene -Dallas Jenkin.
Type in URL: <u>tinyurl.com/pool-of-bethesda</u> (9:56 min.)

Notes: *Other Videos:*

After watching > discovering > relating,
what slogan would you write or draw on your T-shirt?

Draft concepts:

Final design:

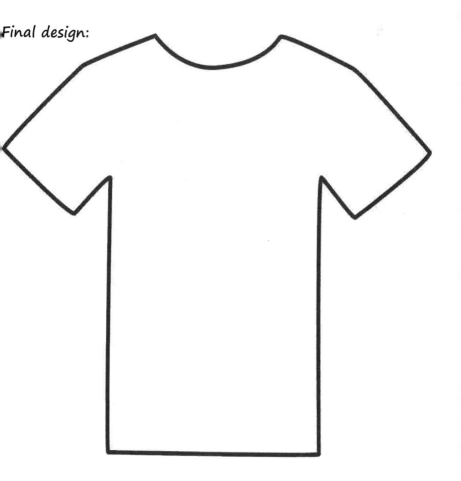

 **Getting ready now for your last gathering.**

Please read the "Prior" note on page 114. If you haven't already done so, work on plans for your last gathering and get it on your group members' schedules, if it is changed from your normal meeting time.

Spirit

INTRO: In *The Chosen*, Season One, we first meet **John the Baptist** when Nicodemus questions him in prison. Due to his dress, eating habits, and life-style (Mark 1:6), Simon called him "Creepy John." But such a description falls quite short of his key role.

No doubt Jesus and John had many interactions over the years, growing up as close-in-age cousins. But The New Testament mentions only their meeting at Jesus' baptism. (For background on the appreciation and respect Jesus held for John and his role in preparing the people for Jesus' coming, see Matthew 11:10-14.)

Find the words that describe John and the words that describe Jesus.

DISCOVER *Read Aloud > Mark It Up > Discuss*

John the Baptist Prepares the Way

MARK 1 The beginning of the gospel of Jesus Christ, the Son of God

² As it is written in Isaiah the prophet,

> Behold, I send my messenger before your face,
>
> who will prepare your way,
>
> ³ the voice of one crying in the wilderness:
>
> 'Prepare the way of the Lord,

⁴ John appeared, baptizing in the wilderness and proclaiming a baptism of repentance for the forgiveness of sins. ⁵ And all the country of Judea and all Jerusalem were going out to him and were being baptized by him in the river Jordan, confessing their sins. ⁶ Now John was clothed with camel's hair and wore a leather belt around his waist and ate locusts and wild honey. ⁷ And he preached, saying, "After me comes he who is mightier than I, the strap of whose sandals I am not worthy to stoop down and untie. ⁸ I have baptized you with water, but he will baptize you with the Holy Spirit."

1. How are John the Baptist and his ministry described?

WATCH *View Episode 5 (45 min., 0:00 to 44:57) > Discuss*

Unlike "Creepy John," a truly creepy guy crawls onto the scene: **Legion**, so-called because of the many demons that possess him. (A Roman *legion* was about 6,000 men.) His screen name is **Caleb**.

2. *What do you find appealing about Jesus' and John's relationship in this episode?*

3. *What strikes you about Mary Magdalene's reactions to the Roman soldier and the demon-possessed man?*

DISCOVER   Read Aloud > Mark It Up > Discuss

INTRO: *The Chosen's* demoniac story is not in the Gospels but has similarities to Mark 5:1-20. Note that Jesus and his disciples are in a Gentile region. **Ask and answer the 'W" questions (see page 12). Look for the action words.**

Jesus Heals a Man with a Demon

Mark 5 They came to the other side of the sea, to the country of the Gerasenes. ² And when Jesus had stepped out of the boat, immediately there met him out of the tombs a man with an unclean spirit. ³ He lived among the tombs. And no one could bind him anymore, not even with a chain, ⁴ for he had often been bound with shackles and chains, but he wrenched the chains apart, and he broke the shackles in pieces. No one had the strength to subdue him. ⁵ Night and day among the tombs and on the mountains, he was always crying out and cutting himself with stones.

⁶ And when he saw Jesus from afar, he ran and fell down before him. ⁷ And crying out with a loud voice, he said, "What have you to do with me, Jesus, Son of the Most High God? I adjure you by God, do not torment me." ⁸ For he was saying to him, "Come out of the man, you unclean spirit!"

⁹ And Jesus asked him, "What is your name?"

He replied, "My name is Legion, for we are many." ¹⁰ And he begged him earnestly not to send them out of the country.

¹¹ Now a great herd of pigs was feeding there on the hillside, ¹²and they begged him, saying, "Send us to the pigs; let us enter them." ¹³ So he gave them permission. And the unclean spirits came out and entered the pigs; and the herd, numbering about two thousand, rushed down the steep bank into the sea and drowned.

¹⁴ The herdsmen fled and told it in the city and in the country. And people came to see what it was that had happened. ¹⁵ And they came to Jesus and saw the demon-possessed man, the one who had had the legion, sitting there, clothed and in his right mind, and they were afraid. ¹⁶ And those who had seen it described to them what had happened to the demon-possessed man and to the pigs. ¹⁷ And they began to beg Jesus to depart from their region.

¹⁸ As he was getting into the boat, the man who had been possessed with demons begged him that he might be with him. ¹⁹ And he did not permit him but said to him, "Go home to your friends and tell them

how much the Lord has done for you, and how he has had mercy on you." [20] And he went away and began to proclaim in the Decapolis how much Jesus had done for him, and everyone marveled.

4. Describe how the demons (Legion) have damaged the man's identity and now must face a "power encounter" with Jesus?

5. Why did the townspeople beg Jesus to leave, and what did they miss as a result?

6. Why do you think Jesus told the man to stay and tell others, when he was eager to go with Jesus and become a disciple (vv. 19-20)?

RELATE | How It Applies to God / Life / You > Discuss

7. What do you miss when you shut Jesus out for other priorities?

NOTES on Study #6 *Commentary and Historical Context*

Mark 1:1-8—John the Baptist Prepares the Way

- John the Baptist was miraculously born to a very old couple (Luke 1:5-80). He had an "Elijah-like ministry" to the Jewish people in order *"to make ready for the Lord a people prepared"* (Luke 1:17).

- John's ministry is closely identified with Elijah (cited in *The Chosen*). Elijah spent six decades (892-832 BD) as a prophet in the northern kingdom, recorded in 1 Kings 17-19 and 2 Kings 1-2. His ministry, not unlike John's, brought him into confrontation with Israel's kings and priests for their contamination of faith in the true God.

  One well-known story pits Elijah against 450 priests of the nature-god, Baal, prized by Ahab and Jezebel. Amidst a country-wide drought, Elijah challenged the priests to a "duel to the death." Suffice it to say, it does not end well for the priests of Baal (see 1 Kings 18:1-40). Elijah was later taken up to heaven in a whirlwind.

  Because Elijah never died and Malachi prophesies his return (4:5-6), some misidentified Jesus as Elijah (Matthew 16:14; Mark 8:28; Luke 9:19). Others thought John could be Elijah. He obviously wasn't. However, John was a *type of Elijah*, who ministered in that prophet's spirit and power (see Luke 1:17). In that respect, Elijah had returned.

John 5:1-15—Jesus Heals a Man with a Demon

- Jesus often *cleansed* people possessed by demons (whereas he *healed* people from disease; see Matthew 7:22; 8:16, 28-34; 9:34; 12:24-28 Mark 1:34; 5:1-20; 16:9). When God's kingdom showed up in Jesus, all hell broke loose—literally.

- Knowing someone's name was thought to give one power over that person, so the demons speak Jesus' name (Mark 5:7). However, this does not work on him and, instead, Jesus commands them.

- The name "Legion" related to the Roman military. Being in a Gentile area with pig farmers (pigs were unclean to Jews, see Deuteronomy 14:8) prompted Jesus to instruct the man not to be quiet, but to tell others. The Gentiles were recipients of God's mercy as well.

• Rome is also put on notice by Jesus' kingdom power. For a two-minute video on how the pigs related to Roman power, or now, lack there-of, see: tinyurl.com/pigs-romans.

That's plausible but did it happen?

Did Simon the Zealot try to knife the demoniac? If he did, it would have been within his character to take such matters into his own hands. While *Caleb* is the screen name of the demon-possessed man (given in *The Chosen*), "Legion" was the name spoken by the demons through him.

In Mark 5 (and Gospel parallels), the demons (Legion), were cast into a herd of 2,000 pigs—animals considered unclean by Jews. The Gentile area (see Decapolis on page 138) is left without this source of income, but not without a Source of Life, in the man's testimony about Jesus.

Did Jesus warn John about the consequences of his actions? Conversely, did John encourage Jesus to take more radical action? Possibly. They were close and pursued a common mission, even if their tactics were different (Luke 7:18-35). John had rebuked Herod for marrying his brother's ex-wife—and was later executed for it—as *The Chosen* foreshadows (see Matthew 14:1-12 and Mark 6:14-29).

At one point John had expressed concern about Jesus' "inaction" and asked for reassurance that Jesus would act (Matthew 11:2-6). Granted, Jesus is vague on specifics of his timing, but he was listening to the Father, a conversation to which John was not a party.

Did the Sanhedrin hold hearings on Jesus and dismiss the charges? The Sanhedrin (the ruling council of 70 Jewish elders) functioned in ways that allowed for this to be a possibility. The Pharisees, who were part of the Sanhedrin, were divided over Jesus; he had a divisive impact on many (John 11:45-57; Acts 4:13-22). Among the Sanhedrin, most opposed Jesus, whereas Nicodemus secretly admired Jesus and argued for fair treatment of him (John 3:1-21; 7:50-52; 19:38-42).

HOME REFLECTION *Journaling, Commitments and Prayer*

Consider this: We live in a fallen world and battle the effects of evil as a result. But, in Jesus, the future of God's total redeeming power invades the present to change us, however imperfectly, into his likeness.

8. *What are some fears, anxieties, struggles with unhealthy choices, relationship challenges, even persistent sin with which you struggle?*

9. So, let that "stuff" out and let Jesus in. *What does it mean to let him in to cleanse, heal, and free you from these issues?*

Video Insight: *Insights from Jesus and the Demoniac*
Type in URL: <u>tinyurl.com/jesus-and-the-demoniac</u> –Mike Winger

Notes: *Other Videos:*   (55:58 min.)

After watching > discovering > relating,
what slogan would you write or draw on your T-shirt?

Draft concepts:

Final design:

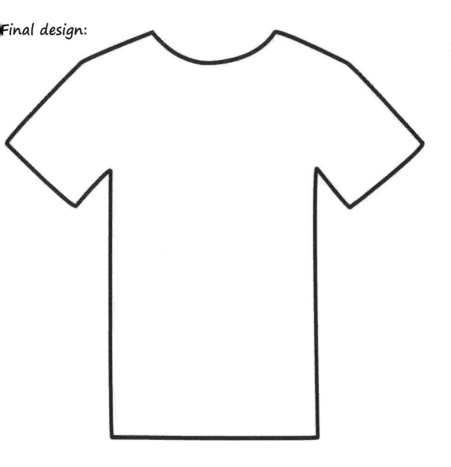

PRIOR
to STUDY

Getting ready for Study #7

NOTE TO EVERYONE: In preparation for this study, you may find it helpful to read the Old Testament account that Jesus refers to in the first passage. It is Samuel 21:1-6 and found below.

David and the Holy Bread

SAMUEL 21 Then David came to Nob, to Ahimelech the priest. And Ahimelech came to meet David, trembling, and said to him, "Why are you alone, and no one with you?"

² And David said to Ahimelech the priest, "The king [Saul] has charged me with a matter and said to me, 'Let no one know anything of the matter about which I send you, and with which I have charged you.' I have made an appointment with the young men for such and such a place. ³ Now then, what do you have on hand? Give me five loaves of bread, or whatever is here."

⁴ And the priest answered David, "I have no common bread on hand, but there is holy bread—if the young men have kept themselves from women."

⁵ And David answered the priest, "Truly women have been kept from us as always when I go on an expedition. The vessels of the young men are holy even when it is an ordinary journey. How much more today will their vessels be holy?"

⁶ So the priest gave him the holy bread, for there was no bread there but the bread of the Presence, which is removed from before the LORD, to be replaced by hot bread on the day it is taken away.

Unlawful

Study #7

FROM The BIBLE

INTRO: In a flashback story, **Ahimelech**, the priest, provides holy bread to **David,** who is running from King Saul (1 Samuel 21:1-6). This "unlawful" precedent was referred to by Jesus 1,000 years later as his disciples faced hunger themselves. The following passages from Mark form the basis for episode six of *The Chosen.*

Look for the words lawful *and* Sabbath *and the attitudes toward them.*

Jesus Is Lord of the Sabbath

MARK 2 [23] One Sabbath he was going through the grain fields, and as they made their way, his disciples began to pluck heads of grain. [24] And the Pharisees were saying to him, "Look, why are they doing what is not lawful on the Sabbath?"

[25] And he said to them, "Have you never read what David did, when he was in need and was hungry, he and those who were with him: [26] how he entered the house of God, in the time of Abiathar the high priest, and ate the bread of the Presence, which it is not lawful for any but the priests to eat, and also gave it to those who were with him?"

[27] And he said to them, "The Sabbath was made for man, not man for the Sabbath. [28] So the Son of Man is lord even of the Sabbath."

A Man with a Withered Hand

MARK 3 Again he entered the synagogue, and a man was there with a withered hand. [2] And they watched Jesus, to see whether he would heal him on the Sabbath, so that they might accuse him. [3] And he said to the man with the withered hand, "Come here."

[4] And he said to them, "Is it lawful on the Sabbath to do good or to do harm, to save life or to kill?" But they were silent.

[5] And he looked around at them with anger, grieved at their hardness of heart, and said to the man, "Stretch out your hand." He stretched it out, and his hand was restored. [6] The Pharisees went out and immediately held counsel with the Herodians against him, how to destroy him.

1. *How does Jesus challenge existing rules about the Sabbath—and why?*

2. *The Pharisees (who opposed Herod) and the Herodians (who supported Herod) are normally mortal enemies, but to thwart Jesus, they form an unholy allegiance (v. 6). How would you contrast what Jesus does on the Sabbath with what they do on the Sabbath?*

WATCH | *View Episode 6 (42 min., from 0:00 to 42:02)* > **Discuss**

INTRO: In this episode we meet three Pharisees: **Dunash, Shmuel** and **Yanni**. They debate the Law as it applies to Jesus, who continues to heal on the Sabbath. Healing **Elam** (the man with the withered hand) is a notable example of this "unlawful"  practice by Jesus. **Madai** and **Lamech,** priests of a small-town synagogue, are aghast at the various ways Jesus violates Jewish tradition regarding the Sabbath.

3. *What situations give rise to the disciples questioning why Jesus doesn't just "fix it"?*

... When have you felt the same way?

DISCOVER Read Aloud > Mark It Up > Discuss

INTRO: Christians under Roman duress (plus any of us who struggle to see God "fix" things) are encouraged to trust God's everlasting love. *Look for the rhetorical questions and their answers.*

FROM The BIBLE

Life in the Spirit

ROMANS 8 There is therefore now no condemnation for those who are in Christ Jesus. ² For the law of the Spirit of life has set you free in Christ Jesus from the law of sin and death....

God's Everlasting Love

ROMANS 8 ³¹ What then shall we say to these things? If God is for us, who can be against us? ³² He who did not spare his own Son but gave him up for us all, how will he not also with him graciously give us all things? ³³ Who shall bring any charge against God's elect? It is God who justifies. ³⁴ Who is to condemn? Christ Jesus is the one who died—more than that, who was raised—who is at the right hand of God, who indeed is interceding for us. ³⁵ Who shall separate us from the love of Christ? Shall tribulation, or distress, or persecution, or famine, or nakedness, or danger, or sword? ³⁶ As it is written,

> "For your sake we are being killed all the day long;
>
> we are regarded as sheep to be slaughtered."

³⁷ No, in all these things we are more than conquerors through him who loved us. ³⁸ For I am sure that neither death nor life, nor angels nor rulers, nor things present nor things to come, nor powers, ³⁹ nor height nor depth, nor anything else in all creation, will be able to separate us from the love of God in Christ Jesus our Lord.

4. What are the far-reaching implications of living under the "law of the Spirit of life" (v. 2)?

5. Trace the steps of Paul's argument for the never-failing love of God.

RELATE How It Applies to God / Life / You > Discuss

6. We can feel unloved, even self-condemned at times. *What does this passage say to those who, like Mary Magdalene, feel this way?*

... *What does this passage mean to you personally?*

7. What is the significance that we are "more than conquerors" (v. 37)?

NOTES on Study #7 *Commentary and Historical Context*

1 Samuel 21:1-6—David and the Holy Bread

- David's request for the "day-old" bread, given to priests after a new batch is made, broke custom, but no laws, regarding worship. Jesus had little concern for such custom.

Mark 2:23–3:6—Jesus Is Lord of the Sabbath

- Jesus urges his disciples to "eat" (not harvest) grain on a Sabbath; this broke no Old Testament law. They were not stealing; the issue regarded what, in Old Testament law, constitutes "prohibited work." The Law permits hungry travelers to eat grain (Deuteronomy 23:25).

- God desires mercy over sacrifice (Hosea 6:6), and the Sabbath is for our full restoration (mental, spiritual, and physical). While Jesus heals on the Sabbath, the Pharisees (Jewish leaders, vehemently opposed to Herod) and the Herodians (Jewish leaders, supportive of Herod)—normally mortal enemies—plot murder on the Sabbath.

Romans 8:1-2—Life in the Spirit

- In Christ, believers live under a "different law," one that frees them from the enslaving power and guilt of sin, which results in spiritual death. "No condemnation" does not allow for God to backtrack on his finished work. "No" means what it says: zero, zilch, none, nada!

- A believer's freedom comes from the rock-solid atoning work of Jesus' death on the Cross as God's sacrificial Lamb. Our circumstances, difficult as they may be, can never circumvent the provision of God's grace in the lives of those who have put their trust in him.

Romans 8:31-39—God's Everlasting Love

- So, what is the extent of Christ's work on our behalf? Paul poses rhetorical questions meant to further affirm the full adequacy of Christ as the gift of God for our complete salvation.

- The Psalmist put into poetry Paul's theology of grace: *As far as the east is from the west,* he declares, *so far has he removed our transgressions from us* (Psalms 103:12). How far away is the east from the west? A very long way!

REALISTIC **But REAL?** That's plausible but did it happen?

Did Mary Magdalene relapse into old habits after her conversion? It's hard to say, but this is the lived experience of every believer who, on his side of heaven, will struggle with sin and temptation. So, it is possible, and lends Jesus a wonderful opportunity to affirm that we have a great salvation in him which cannot be lost.

Did Matthew and Simon pair up to find Mary who had lost her way? This story isn't part of the New Testament record. But if we hypothesize that Mary "lost her way," you can be sure Jesus would do anything and everything to find her. That he sent two disparate messengers of hope—who would also get something out of learning to work together—adds a natural, plausible dimension to the story.

HOME REFLECTION Journaling, Commitments and Prayer

8. *When did you first become aware of God's love for you? Describe.*

9. *How have you struggled to believe the full extent of God's love for you?*

... What aspects of God's love does Romans 8 bring to mind for you?

Video Insight: Who is Simon (and Matthew) Becoming?

Type in URL: <u>tinyurl.com/simon-and-matthew</u> –Brandon Snipe

Notes: **Other Videos:**   (16:13 min.)

After watching > discovering > relating,
what slogan would you write or draw on your T-shirt?

Draft concepts:

Final design:

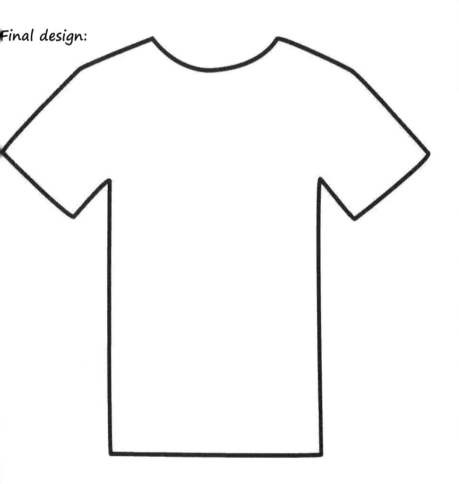

 **Getting ready for your last gathering.**

Please read the "Prior" note on page 116. If you haven't already done so, finalize your plans for your last gathering to get it on your group members' schedules, if it is changed from your normal meeting time.

Reckoning

INTRO: Herod's wife, **Herodias,** is angry at John the Baptist for denouncing their marriage as unlawful (see Matthew 14:1-12). So John is arrested by **Herod** and languishes in prison. His imprisonment put Jesus' disciples on edge regarding his fate, as well as that of their own rabbi.

In this episode of *The Chosen*, an arrest of Jesus by Roman authorities starts to prepare his disciples to trust and obey him, even when he is not physically present. Before his death, Jesus will similarly make clear to his disciples that the Holy Spirit will come into their lives as their helper, replacing his physical presence.

John 14 describes this ongoing presence of God the Father, Spirit, and the Son in the lives of his followers. Not only could Jesus' immediate disciples take comfort in his reassurances, so can his disciples in all times and places.

Look for all of the promises given in this passage.

DISCOVER   *Read Aloud > Mark It Up > Discuss*

JOHN 14:15-21 & 25-27, Jesus Promises the Holy Spirit

[15] "If you love me, you will keep my commandments. [16] And I will ask the Father, and he will give you another Helper, to be with you forever, [17] even the Spirit of truth, whom the world cannot receive because it neither sees him nor knows him. You know him, for he dwells with you and will be in you.

[18] "I will not leave you as orphans; I will come to you. [19] Yet a little while and the world will see me no more, but you will see me. Because I live, you also will live. [20] In that day you will know that I am in my Father, and you in me, and I in you. [21] Whoever has my commandments and keeps them, he it is who loves me. And he who loves me will be loved by my Father, and I will love him and manifest myself to him....

[25] "These things I have spoken to you while I am still with you. [26] But the Helper, the Holy Spirit, whom the Father will send in my name, he will teach you all things and bring to your remembrance all that I have said to you. [27] Peace I leave with you; my peace I give to you. Not as the world gives do I give to you. Let not your hearts be troubled, neither let them be afraid.

1. *What does Jesus promise his followers for the time when he would not physically present with them?*

2. How does Jesus describe the character and role of the Holy Spirit?

3. What does Jesus say it takes to be in a love relationship with him?

WATCH   View Episode 7 (41 min., from 0:00 to 40:26) > **Discuss**

INTRO: **Tamar**, the Ethiopian woman who wit-
nesssed two healings in Season One, is joined by
her formerly paralyzed friend. They boldly give
their testimony to a crowd, reporting what they

saw and experienced firsthand of Jesus' power to heal and restore.

Quintus and **Atticus**, the Roman magistrates from Season One,
are concerned with Jesus' irregularities. They have Jesus arrested, to
the great concern of his disciples, as he is led away for interrogation.

4. How does Jesus provide an example of submitting to authorities?

5. Note the disciples' responses around the daytime campfire. *Which
of their reactions would characterize yours in that situation—and why?*

DISCOVER *Read Aloud > Mark It Up > Discuss*

INTRO: This version of the Lord's Prayer (the other is in *The Sermon on the Mount*, Matthew 6:4-14) is in response to the disciples' request, *Lord, teach us to pray.* Jesus proceeds to give them a general  model for prayer life. ***Look for the elements in Jesus' prayer as well as cause and effect in the illustrations that follow.***

The Lord's Prayer

LUKE 11 Now Jesus was praying in a certain place, and when he finished, one of his disciples said to him, "Lord, teach us to pray, as John taught his disciples." ² And he said to them, "When you pray, say:

"Father,

hallowed be your name.

Your kingdom come.

³ Give us each day our daily bread,

⁴ and forgive us our sins,

for we ourselves forgive everyone who is indebted to us.

And lead us not into temptation."

⁵ And he said to them, "Which of you who has a friend will go to him at midnight and say to him, 'Friend, lend me three loaves, ⁶ for a friend of mine has arrived on a journey, and I have nothing to set before him'; ⁷ and he will answer from within, 'Do not bother me; the door is now shut, and my children are with me in bed. I cannot get up and give you anything'? ⁸ I tell you, though he will not get up and give him anything because he is his friend, yet because of his impudence he will rise and give him whatever he needs.

And I tell you, ask, and it will be given to you; seek, and you will find; knock, and it will be opened to you. [10] For everyone who asks receives, and the one who seeks finds, and to the one who knocks it will be opened.

[11] What father among you, if his son asks for a fish, will instead of a fish give him a serpent; [12] or if he asks for an egg, will give him a scorpion? [13] If you then, who are evil, know how to give good gifts to your children, how much more will the heavenly Father give the Holy Spirit to those who ask him!"

6. Note each element of Jesus' model prayer. *How is each one vital in a love relationship with God and others:*

... *Father ("Abba": literally, Daddy, see page 100)?*

... *Hallowed be your name?*

... *Your kingdom come?*

... *Give us each day our daily bread?*

... *Forgive us our sins?*

... *For we ourselves forgive everyone who is indebted to us?*

... *Lead us not into temptation?*

7. *How is prayer to the Lord similar to waking the friend who is in bed?*

8. *How is God like a father who gives gifts to his children?*

RELATE | How It Applies to God / Life / You > Discuss

9. *What in Jesus' teaching on prayer is most meaningful to you right now?*

NOTES on Study #8 *Commentary and Historical Context*

JOHN 14:15-21 & 25-27—Jesus Promises the Holy Spirit

- The Trinity (the unity of Father, Son, and Holy Spirit as three persons in one God) shows up in a big way in Jesus' teaching here.

- His leaving is not something to be feared but embraced as the means to experience the full measure of God's presence in their lives through the Holy Spirit. He will not leave those who love and obey him as *orphans but* promises his abundant peace.

Luke 11:1-11—The Lord's Prayer

- Each Jewish group had their own distinctive way of praying, including those following John the Baptist. Jesus' disciples wanted to learn his way of praying. He gives them a model of key elements to use.

- The word for Father, *Abba*, is the most intimate word a child could use: *Daddy*. The Jews would only speak God's title, *Adonai*, not his personal name, *Yahweh*, believing it too holy to utter. Not so for Jesus' followers. Jesus' sacrifice makes a way for us to know God in the most intimate of ways: as a child to a loving dad or mom.

The rationale in the Lord's Prayer, *for we also forgive* (v. 4), reminds us that God's forgiveness produces the willingness to forgive.

That's plausible but did it happen?

Before his crucifixion, was Jesus arrested and interrogated by Roman officials?

The members of the Sanhedrin (the ruling council of 70 Jewish elders) were not the only ones curious about and divided over Jesus; the Jews feared intervention by Roman rulers if things got out of hand (John 11:45-48). The Romans would tolerate no actions that might threaten their rule.

The arrest of Jesus in the Garden of Gethsemane (Matthew 26:36) and his subsequent trial, lead some to believe that this was not the first time that Jesus had problems with the legal authorities. His example of humbly submitting to authorities gave rise to the disciples' worries (in *The Chosen*), and their request for a teaching on prayer.

HOME REFLECTION *Journaling, Commitments and Prayer*

Prayer can be discouraging when you see little or no results for your efforts. Jesus encourages perseverance (Luke 11:9-10):

> [9] *And I tell you, ask, and it will be given to you; seek, and you will find; knock, and it will be opened to you.* [10] *For everyone who asks receives, and the one who seeks finds, and to the one who knocks it will be opened.*

The verbs here indicate a continual practice: keep on asking, keep on knocking, keep on asking.

10. *If you don't continue asking, what does that reveal about your view of God?*

11. *How has (or could) continued prayer change you and change the things for which you ask?*

Video Insight: The Lord's Prayer, A Teaching Moment
Type in URL: tinyurl.com/lords-prayer-teaching-moment (5:18 min.)

Notes: **Other Videos:**   –Rabbi Jason Sobel

After watching > discovering > relating,
what slogan would you write or draw on your T-shirt?

Draft concepts:

Final design:

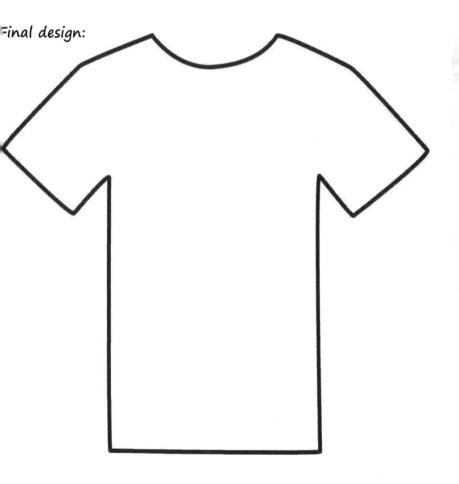

 A beautiful and meaningful Psalm

NOTE TO EVERYONE: Before this gathering, take time to read and reflect on the passage Matthew, Philip, Ramah, and Mary Magdalene were finding comfort in and direction from. The sections they reference are shown in bold in Psalm 139 (pages 107-109).

Beyond Mountains

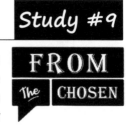

Study #9

INTRO: A landowner is swindled by a businessman and his apprentice. The two go on to help the disciples negotiate a "price" for a place to host a major teaching by Jesus. That teaching we know as *The Sermon on the Mount*.

The apprentice involved in the swindle turns out to be, well, we won't spoil it for you. Some of the disciples' families and friends from Season One also appear in this last scene, to reconnect and hear Jesus' message.

WATCH View Episode 8 (44 min., from 2:37 to 46:30) > Discuss

1. *Describe:*
... the feelings of the disciples around camp.

... the resistance to Jesus by Shmuel, Yanni and other Pharisees.

... the negotiation for using the land for Jesus' sermon.

... the choosing of sash color to accessorize Jesus.

2. In the film, Judas is the last disciple to appear on the scene. *Was he someone who you might expect to be Judas? Why or why not?*

DISCOVER Read Aloud > Mark It Up > Discuss

INTRO: In episodes 2 and 3 Matthew, Ramah, and Mary Magdalene become interested in the study of Scripture. Philip introduces **Psalm 139:8** for meditation and, in the episode, Mary helps Ramah to read using **Psalm 139: 15-16** (in bold below). *Identify each section and give each a title.*

FROM *The* BIBLE

To the choirmaster. A Psalm of David.

Psalm 139 O LORD, you have searched me and known me!

2 You know when I sit down and when I rise up;

you discern my thoughts from afar.

3 You search out my path and my lying down

and are acquainted with all my ways.

4 Even before a word is on my tongue,

behold, O LORD, you know it altogether.

5 You hem me in, behind and before,

and lay your hand upon me.

6 Such knowledge is too wonderful for me;

it is high; I cannot attain it.

7 Where shall I go from your Spirit?

Or where shall I flee from your presence?

8 **If I ascend to heaven, you are there!**

If I make my bed in Sheol, you are there!

9 If I take the wings of the morning

and dwell in the uttermost parts of the sea,

10 even there your hand shall lead me,

and your right hand shall hold me.

11 If I say, "Surely the darkness shall cover me,

and the light about me be night,"

12 even the darkness is not dark to you;

the night is bright as the day,

for darkness is as light with you.

¹³ For you formed my inward parts;

you knitted me together in my mother's womb.

¹⁴ I praise you, for I am fearfully and wonderfully made.

Wonderful are your works;

my soul knows it very well.

¹⁵ My frame was not hidden from you,

when I was being made in secret,

intricately woven in the depths of the earth.

¹⁶ Your eyes saw my unformed substance;

in your book were written, every one of them,

the days that were formed for me,

when as yet there was none of them.

¹⁷ How precious to me are your thoughts, O God!

How vast is the sum of them!

¹⁸ If I would count them, they are more than the sand.

I awake, and I am still with you.

¹⁹ Oh that you would slay the wicked, O God!

O men of blood, depart from me!

²⁰ They speak against you with malicious intent;

your enemies take your name in vain.

²¹ Do I not hate those who hate you, O LORD?

And do I not loathe those who rise up against you?

²² I hate them with complete hatred;

I count them my enemies.

²³ Search me, O God, and know my heart!

Try me and know my thoughts!

²⁴ And see if there be any grievous way in me,

and lead me in the way everlasting!

3. *Which parts of the Psalm stand out to you?*

4. *How well, or to what extent, does our Creator God know us?*

... How does David express his feelings about God's ever-presence?

5. *What does it means to be "knitted together" and "fearfully and wonderfully made" (vv. 13-14)?*

... Why, though, do we doubt this about ourselves?

6. In verses 19-22, David addresses "the wicked." *Why do you think he expresses such passion against them?*

7. *How would you compare the kind of searching and knowledge the Psalm begins with (vv. 1-6) to the kind cited at the end (vv. 23-24)?*

RELATE   How It Applies to God / Life / You > Discuss

8. *What do you expect would happen in and through your life, if you regularly prayed like verses 23-24?*

9. *What do you think God is seeking to show you right now through making this prayer your heartfelt request?*

NOTES on Study #9 *Commentary and Historical Context*

Psalm 139—Psalm of David on the Presence of God

- David did not have a deep understanding of the person of God as manifested in the Father, Son, and Holy Spirit. He wasn't, obviously, in the upper room with the disciples, so he would not have heard Jesus describe what makes for a continued, intimate relationship with him and the Father. He would know nothing of the Holy Spirit's presence as revealed in our last study from John 14.

  Neither would David, like his fellow Old Testament Jews, have called on God in such intimate terms as did Jesus. In the Lord's Prayer, Jesus directed his disciples to address God as *Abba*— "Daddy". (The Jews would only speak God's title, *Adonai*, not his name: *Yahweh*.)

  But David was *a man after God's own heart*. He describes, in poetic words, the cherished familiarity Jesus' followers have with their God, as one redeemed and adopted into his family.

- The Scripture passage in *The Chosen* that Phillip, Matthew, Mary, and Ramah memorized and meditated on, is Psalm 139:8. This verse uses the Greek term, *Sheol,* or *the depths*. The term is not *Hell* (Gehenna) used in Matthew 10:28. Instead it indicates the utter depths of this world—*the grave.*

  Up or down, near or far, early or late, day or night—wherever we go, God is with us all the time, all the way. Our finite minds cannot grasp how awesome, how wonderful and "how everywhere" God is.

- The fact that God knows and cares for us in the womb before being born (vv. 13-16) indicates that he is concerned for life at the moment of conception. David had no clue as to the intricacies of the body that modern science has revealed. All he had was his ability to marvel! Whatever your stance on the issue of abortion, allow these verses to inform your thinking and practice.

- Psalm 139 reminds us of just how worthy of worship God is, how inappropriate it is not to acknowledge him (vv. 17-22), and how open we should be for him to teach and lead us further (vv. 23-24).

 *That's plausible but did it happen?*

Was Judas (Iscariot) an apprentice and swindler in sales, yet ambitious for a life of purpose?
Such backstory is quite speculative. Judas would have made a likely compatriot for Simon the Zealot. The Gospels, however, give us no background on either of them, other than what we can glean from their names and, in Judas' case, his actions.

Simon (the Zealot), similar to Judas Iscariot, likely had a strong vision of what it could mean to join forces with the new Jesus Movement. But while Simon became a true believer, Judas, sadly, never made such a wholehearted commitment. Why he would not forsake his independent ambitions to be transformed by his relationship with Jesus remains a mystery.

Did Jesus dress plainly?
In *The Chosen,* Jesus whimsically alludes to Isaiah 53:2, and chides the women trying to dress him up: *You know I know what the prophecy says about my appearance. Is this your attempt to change it?* True, nothing about Jesus' appearance commended him. Leave it to the key women in his entourage, though, to adorn him for the big occasion! Royal blue gets a tie-breaking vote to accessorize the *Prince of Peace.*

Was Jesus a revolutionary?
By all accounts, yes. His followers would have him subvert Rome, and his critics are concerned he just might. Jesus himself (in *The Chosen*) clarifies that his message is not meant to be soothing or sentimental; rather, he intends to "start a revolution, but not a revolt." That distinction makes all the difference, as we shall see.

Many Scriptures, in both Old and New Testaments, support this claim, but none more than the *Sermon on the Mount,* which is a manifesto, radical for its day, and ours! We'll learn more about it in Season 3.

10. Read over Psalm 139 in personal terms. *What do you appreciate about its description regarding God's intimate knowledge of you?*

11. *Embrace verses 23-24 as a model for your own request by rewriting and expanding these words for your own life with God, the Father, his Son, and the Holy Spirit.*

Video Insight: Dallas Gives Speech for The Chosen –Dallas Jenkins
Type in URL: tinyurl.com/dallas-speech (3:30 min.)

Notes: **Other Videos:**

After watching > discovering > relating, what slogan would you write or draw on your T-shirt?

Draft concepts:

Final design:

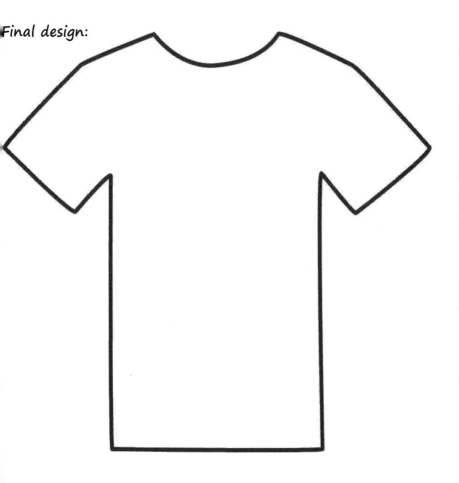

Time to put it all together

-*The tenth meeting* includes a review of Season Two, a bridge to Season Three, and reflection on what we've learned and experienced so far.

Note: For this gathering, your group could meet at your normal time, or as an alternative, you could plan to meet in a special place for a longer event which can do wonders as a group bonding experience. **Pages 125-132** can be used for an *extended Home Reflection* time, for a *Day-Long event* or a *Weekend retreat.*

See page 15 for an overview of a **Day-Long Event** or **Weekend Retreat.** thechosenstudy.org, under *Leaders* has further suggestions as well.

It is a priority to have as many in your group come as possible, hopefully everyone, no matter what you do! So, discuss options and get it on your group members' schedule, as early as possible.

Hopefully, you and your group will want to continue the Chosen experience and invite new people to your next study!

-*For this study re-watch two film clips from episode 8.* Be ready for their presentation.

Integrate Your Chosen Experience

Season Two Reviewed and Looking Ahead **Study #10**

INTRO: The cover on this guide illustrates the centrality of hope for our journey. Counterfeit hope lurks all around and markets its wares to us with a superficial offer of peace, contentment, and joy.

But the superficial things, in which we place our hope, fail to acknowledge that we all have a "God-shaped void." This is a void only Jesus and his kingdom values can satisfy. This will be made even more evident in his famous and provocative message (Matthew 5-7). Here we watch *The Chosen's* preview of its introduction, then review its introduction (the Beatitudes) ourselves.

RE-WATCH Episode 8B (21:18–27:27 & 32:53–36:32) > Discuss

1. As you consider the disciples' camp with Jesus, what inspiring examples of "blessedness" stood out for you and why?

2. In *The Chosen,* Jesus calls his opening "a map, directions where people should look to find me." *In what respect can The Beatitudes be used as a map to find him?*

DISCOVER Read Aloud > Mark It Up > Discuss

INTRO: The Big Reveal of Jesus' counter-cultural message begins with a series of statements on "blessedness." Let your imagination soar as you hear the words, either for the first time or afresh.

Look for the contrasts in the passage and the analogies in vv. 13-14.

The Sermon on the Mount
MATTHEW 5 Seeing the crowds, he went up on the mountain, and when he sat down, his disciples came to him.

The Beatitudes
² And he opened his mouth and taught them, saying:

³ "Blessed are the poor in spirit,

for theirs is the kingdom of heaven.

⁴ "Blessed are those who mourn,

for they shall be comforted.

[5] "Blessed are the meek,

> for they shall inherit the earth.

[6] "Blessed are those who hunger and thirst for righteousness,

> for they shall be satisfied.

[7] "Blessed are the merciful,

> for they shall receive mercy.

[8] "Blessed are the pure in heart,

> for they shall see God.

[9] "Blessed are the peacemakers,

> for they shall be called sons of God.

[10] "Blessed are those who are persecuted for righteousness' sake,

> for theirs is the kingdom of heaven.

[12] Rejoice and be glad, for your reward is great in heaven, for so

> they persecuted the prophets who were before you.

Salt and Light

[13] "You are the salt of the earth, but if salt has lost its taste, how shall its saltiness be restored? It is no longer good for anything except to be thrown out and trampled under people's feet.

[14] "You are the light of the world. A city set on a hill cannot be hidden.

3. *What would you say it means to be "blessed," according to Jesus?*

4. *What does Jesus mean when he identifies his followers as salt and light? (vv. 13-14)*

5. **Read aloud:** Sometimes the best way to understand a truth is by its opposite. The "eight blessings" (the eighth is a two-parter) are divided on this page and the next. **Have each person write out their opposites,** *The Be-Notitudes,* and **then share them in the group.**

   The Beatitudes are Kingdom of God values that Jesus says will ensure that we are happy and content.

   The Be-Notitudes are Kingdom of the World values. They tempt us to believe that, by living accordingly, we will be happy and content.

The Beatitudes and The "Be-Notitudes"	
Kingdom of God values	**Kingdom of the World values**
³ *"Blessed are the poor in spirit, for theirs is the kingdom of heaven.*	Example: *Happy are the proud and boastful who never pursue humility because they never need to admit wrong and are totally self-sufficient.*
⁴ *"Blessed are those who mourn, for they shall be comforted.*	
⁵ *"Blessed are the meek, for they shall inherit the earth.*	

[5] *"Blessed are those who hunger and thirst for righteousness, for they shall be satisfied.*	Example: *Secure are those who work hard for their possessions, fame, position and power, for they will get all they want.*
[7] *"Blessed are the merciful, for they shall receive mercy.*	
[8] *"Blessed are the pure in heart, for they shall see God.*	
[9] *"Blessed are the peacemakers, for they shall be called sons of God.*	Example: *Content are those who can manipulate and play people off each other for they will get their needs met without being sincere.*
[10] *"Blessed are those who are persecuted for righteousness' sake, for theirs is the kingdom of heaven.*	
[11] *"Blessed are you when others revile you and persecute you and utter all kinds of evil against you falsely on my account.* [12] *Rejoice and be glad, for your reward is great in heaven, for so they persecuted the prophets who were before you.*	

6. *After writing (including the ones with examples, if you'd like), read each aloud. Then "vote" on the best examples. Have fun with it!*

7. How was looking at the opposites of The Beatitudes helpful?

8. Which Be-Notitudes helped you to see their opposite better?

RELATE How It Applies to God / Life / You > Discuss

9. Which Be-Notitudes are you most likely to pursue?

10. What can you do to "salt up" or bring "more light" into the world?

11. *Which friends, neighbors, co-workers, and/or family members do you sense God would have you help (as salt and light) through service, prayer, and dialogue about spiritual things?*

-         -   -

-         -   -

-         -   -

12. *Can you envision using* The Chosen *film and* The Chosen *Study as a means of inviting people into a dialogue about Jesus? Explain.*

13. *Could you imagine yourself going a step further by facilitating a one-to-one experience or a group? If so, how? And with whom?*

Note: Please consider *Our Mission—Our Team—Our Invitation* on page 155. We'd love to have you join with us: <u>thechosenstudy.org/join</u>.

NOTES on Study #10	*Commentary and Historical Context*

Matthew 5:1-14—The Beatitudes, Salt and Light

- These eight statements begin with the English word, *blessed*, which in Latin is *beatus*, giving us the origin of the name Beatitudes.

- "Blessed are" is not to say that the poor, meek, mournful, or hungry are happy or prospering. Rather, they are to be congratulated or considered fortunate for living with the spiritual values that reflect a right relationship with God and reject counterfeit fulfillment.

- Salt, as a metaphor for a Christ-follower, underscores our place in society as adding value and flavor, keeping the good from going bad. Salt never loses its saltiness except when diluted with water. By this analogy, a "useless" (salt-less) Christian is one diluted by worldly influences, rather than salting up or influencing the world.

- Light is another useful analogy for the Jesus-follower. A small candle or flashlight fills and lights up an otherwise dark room; its small light is not overcome by darkness. A "flashdark," if there were such a thing, is powerless compared to a flashlight. Only light kept hidden under a bowl loses its effective, illuminating outreach.

HOME REFLECTION | *Looking back and looking forward*

14. **Read through pages 133-135** regarding the Gospels' authors and characters. *What surprised, encouraged, or challenged you about their stories?*

    –

    –

    –

    –

15. *Where would you have placed yourself on this continuum (put a smaller x) regarding your relationship with God/Jesus when you began this study (on page 41)? Where are you now (put a larger X)?*

Observer…   Skeptic…   Learner…   Seeker…   Follower…

16. What new spiritual perspective do you have about God/Jesus/
direction in your life/other?

-

-

-

-

Video Insights: From Atheist to The Chosen's Sermon on the
Mount scene –Anna

Type in URL: tinyurl.com/atheist-to-follower (5:26 min.)

Notes: **Other Videos:**

After watching > discovering > relating,
what slogan would you write or draw on your T-shirt?

Draft concepts:

Final design:

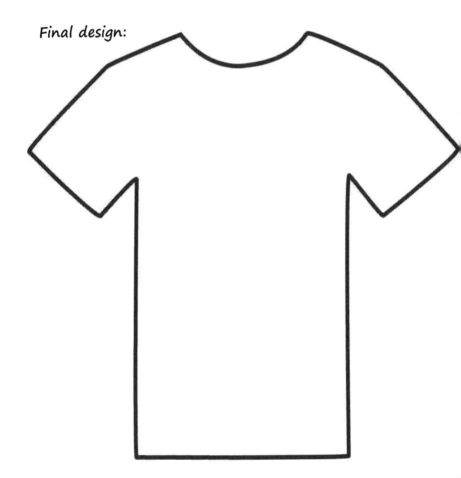

Your Faith Journey

Best takeaways for:

- -An Extended Home Reflection
- -A Day-Long Event
- -A Weekend Retreat (See page 15 for these.)

#1, I Am He / Thunder:

#2, Thunder:

#3, I Saw You:

#4, Matthew 4:24:

#5, The Perfect Opportunity:

More takeaways: (Longer events can use video clips: See website.)

#6, Spirit:

#7, Unlawful:

#8, Reckoning:

#9, Beyond Mountains:

#10, Integrate Your Chosen Experience:

Read this definition of faith and "Mark It Up!"

The Chosen is meant to take you into the eyes and ears of the people who followed Jesus. We believe that if you can see Jesus through the eyes of those who met him, you can be changed and impacted in the same way they were.... If we can connect you with their burdens and struggles and questions, then ideally, we can connect you to the solution, to the answer to those questions. —Dallas Jenkins

One definition of genuine faith is *giving all you know about yourself to all you know about God.* Such is the call to humility. And the more you hang around Jesus, the more you realize that he isn't impressed with pretension. Maybe that's why he—the Servant-King, God's understated Messiah—made no grand entry. Instead, Jesus shows up as a baby, born in a dirty stable to a peasant girl, in a nondescript town.

Then, 30 years later, for three short years, he announces that the Kingdom of God has arrived, complete with spiritually intriguing stories and miracles. He offers forgiveness of sin, and reconciliation to God the Father—all culminating in his crucifixion, resurrection, and ascension.

Something is going on here. No one could make this stuff up. If nothing more, **the story of Jesus is the most [_____ fill in the blank] story that humanity has ever offered**. The Gospel writers certainly felt this way and their eagerness to describe this off-the-charts, unusual *eternity-meets-time event* pours through their various accounts.

From your study, **write in the adjective** *that best describes Jesus' story?*

  Remarkable . . .

    Compelling . . .

      Audacious . . .

        Captivating . . .

No fair picking them all!   Fascinating . . .

We chose one—what's yours?   Intriguing. . .

Share why you selected it with your group.   Other . . .

Watch > Discover > Relate the Most _____ *Story Ever Told.*

Do you increasingly find yourself caught up in Jesus' story, as well? Do you want it, and him, to influence your life more deeply? Then, take on what you learn. If Jesus says to love your enemies, try it out. Or, if he says to show hospitality like the Good Samaritan, or to help find lost sheep like a Good Shepherd, then do it.

As you "try on Jesus' teaching," you will find it not only making sense, but that you will also need to look to him for the wisdom, strength, and courage to take the risk of making some hard choices. Thankfully, in this journey of faith, his forgiveness is always close at hand.

1. *How have you connected with the above quote by Dallas?*

2. *How do you respond to the definition of faith given on page 129?*

3. *Which teaching of Jesus would God have you "try on" right now?*

4. *With whom can you share what you've learned and its impact on you?*

Faith Journey Notes:

Have you seen something different in Jesus?

Join a Chosen Study Team and consider becoming a

Chosen Study Leader

More Notes:

Background Notes Where his story came from

Early tradition identifies Matthew, Mark, Luke, and John as the ones who introduced Jesus to the First Century world and to ours. Their portrait of him is both historically unique and remarkably consistent.

MATTHEW: Given his occupation as a tax collector for the Roman government, we can only imagine the initial tension between Matthew (also called Levi) and the other disciples. But reconciliation lay at the heart of Jesus' message (see *The Sermon on the Mount,* Mathew 5-7). Matthew's Gospel emphasizes the interconnectedness between the Old and New Testaments and provides young believers a systematic tutorial on Jesus' teaching.

MARK: This Gospel has been generally recognized as the account coming from Peter. Mark begins his first "sentence" with no verb: *The beginning of the Gospel about Jesus Christ, the Son of God.* His last sentence ends with the women fleeing Jesus' empty tomb *because they were afraid.* For Mark, Jesus is a man of action. To help believers facing persecution from the Roman state, Mark focuses on Jesus as the Suffering Servant who "came to serve" (Mark 10:45).

LUKE: An educated Greek physician and traveling companion of Paul, Luke authored the book of Acts and the Gospel that bears his name. Although Luke never met Jesus himself, he had a close relationship with Paul, and was acquainted with most of the key eyewitnesses who knew Jesus (Luke 1:1-4). After extensive interviews with these contacts, Luke begins: "Since I myself have carefully investigated everything from the beginning, it seemed good also to me to write an orderly account" (Luke 1:3).

JOHN: A fisherman and brother of James, he writes, "In the beginning was the Word," offering a rather obvious parallel to the opening words of Genesis. In the "first Genesis," God spoke *Creation* into existence, and in the "second Genesis" God speaks *Redemption* into existence: "The Word became flesh and made his dwelling among us" (1:14). This "Word made flesh" is who John wants his readers to know.

Knowing those who knew him best

Mary Magdalene: One of several women mentioned in Luke 8:2-3 who had been "cured of evil spirits and diseases" and was following Jesus. Having been delivered from seven demons, she is with Jesus at the cross and is the first one to whom Jesus appears after the Crucifixion (Luke 8:2-3; John 19:25-27; John 20:1-18).

John the Baptist: Miraculously conceived shortly before his cousin Jesus, he heralds Jesus, as foretold by Isaiah (40:3-5), calling Jews to repent in preparation for the Messiah. After a faithful ministry and baptizing Jesus, he is imprisoned and later beheaded for the threat he posed to Herod Antipas. Jesus identifies him as *the greatest of those born of women* (John 1:6-34; Matthew 3:1-17; 11:1-19; 14:1-12; Luke 1:5-25, 57-80).

Andrew: One of the first to follow Jesus, he brings his brother, Simon (Peter), right away. Together with fellow fishermen, James and John, Andrew leaves everything to follow Jesus after the miraculous catch. He also plays a key role in the feeding of the 5,000 (John 1:40-42; 6:8-9).

Simon: This fisherman meets Jesus and is later renamed Peter, *the Rock*. He is brought to Jesus by his brother, Andrew, and follows Jesus thereafter. He is well-known for walking (and sinking) on water, slicing off a soldier's ear, denying Jesus before his death, being a prominent leader in the early Christian movement, and for writing 1 and 2 Peter (Matthew 14:25-32; 16:13-28; Mark 14:66-72; John 1:40-42; Luke 5:1-11).

James and John: Along with Simon, they become Jesus' closest disciples. Appropriately nicknamed by Jesus as the "sons of thunder" (Luke 9:54), they were Simon's partners and, like him, they left everything to follow Jesus after the huge catch of fish (Mark 3:17; Luke 5:1-11). John goes on to write a Gospel, three letters, and the Book of Revelation.

Matthew: Also known as Levi, is a despised tax collector when Jesus calls him from his tax booth to follow Him. He *left everything and followed him,* and invites many friends and coworkers to a dinner with Jesus (Luke 5:27-32). He authors the Gospel of Matthew.

James the Less (*micros,* meaning "little" or "young") and **Thaddeus:** Two lesser-known disciples: "Little James," a son of Alphaeus (Mark 3:18), could have been Matthew's brother (also a son of Alphaeus, Mark 2:14), but is never identified as such. Thaddeus, aka Jude/Judas, may have gotten his nickname (meaning "breast child" or "mama's boy") to distinguish him from the other Judas, to avoid negative connotations.

Thomas (aka Didymus, or "twin"): Best known for doubting: *Unless I see the nail marks in his hands... I will not believe* (John 20:25). Thomas could, maybe more accurately, be called *logical*. Regardless, we see a whole-hearted passion, even an openness to die with Jesus (11:16), and fear of missing him (14:5). Thomas, the last of The Twelve to see Jesus after the resurrection, upon seeing him proclaims, *My Lord and my God* (20:24-29).

Mary, mother of Jesus: She is the teenager God chose to give birth to Jesus, who was conceived in her by the Holy Spirit. She raises Jesus with **Joseph,** who married her after an angel appears to him in a dream, and who probably died before Jesus began his adult ministry. She weeps at the Crucifixion, witnesses the resurrected Christ, and, along with at least some of her other children (Acts 1:14), is part of the early church (Luke 1:26-56; 2:5-7; 8:19-21; John 2:1-12; 19:25-27).

Philip is a disciple of John the Baptist, and a friend of Andrew. He changes allegiance from John to Jesus, and seeks out a friend, **Nathanael,** who wonders aloud, *Can anything good come out of Nazareth?* Philp seemingly quotes Jesus, *Come and see!* Nathanael does and is amazed that Jesus "met him" before they meet: *Before Philip called you, when you were under the fig tree, I saw you.*

Simon (the Zealot) is distinct from Simon (Peter). We don't know a lot about him from the gospel record other than his association with the Zealots, a group of Jewish insurrectionists who opposed Roman rule. Without much to go on, there has been a wide variety of speculation. Some options are: the same person as Simeon of Jerusalem who became an early Christian leader, Simon, the brother of Jesus, perhaps a cousin of Jesus, or even a son of Joseph from a previous marriage.

Judas (Iscariot)—was a name probably given to him as a designation of his native place, Kerioth, a town in Judah. In *The Chosen* he is introduced as the last of the disciples to join, but the New Testament only indicates that he was one of the Twelve, not when he joined.

Spoiler Alert! What happens next . . .

Episode 1: *Waiting for Season Three to drop.*

Episode 2: *Hey, we're not clairvoyant!*

Episode 3: *And we have no special pipeline to Dallas Jenkins!!*

Episode 4: *However, we'll go out on a limb here and say it will include the Sermon on the Mount. So, get ready by studying Matthew 5-7!!!*

Episode 5:

Episode 6:

Episode 7:

Episode 8:

Mark where it happened on the map (Bible-History.com)

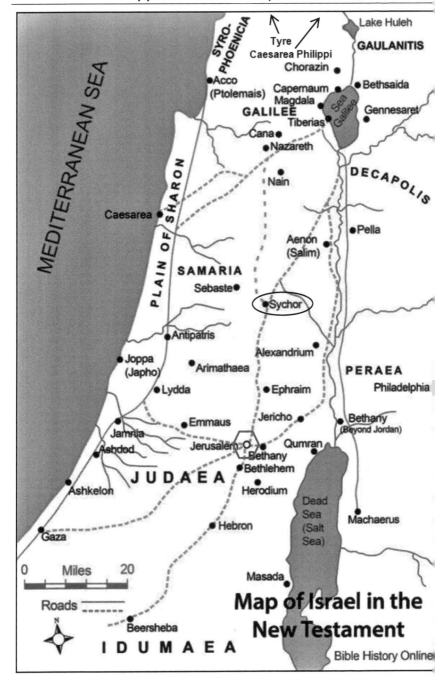

Record locations cited and what happened there:

– Sychar, Samaria: John 4:39, woman at the well (p. 36)

–

–

–

–

–

–

–

Bible apps and online access

The **You Version** app, installed on over 500 million devices, is used on smartphones and tablets, and accessed online at bible.com and youversion.com. Excellent for reading.

Bible Gateway is a searchable online Bible in more than 200 versions and 70 languages that can be read and referenced online at biblegateway.com. Excellent for researching.

BibleProject.com and app, used in Study #1, includes a high-quality collection of videos on books of the Bible, biblical themes, and word studies. Excellent for learning.

100% FREE: The Life and Teachings of Jesus of Nazareth

Would you like a compilation of the four Gospels for yourself and to give away? Order free (224 pages, shipping included) at plusnothing.com.

Can you trust The Chosen?

Some have raised questions about the authenticity of *The Chosen—* which is what this guide's *Realistic But Real?* sections highlight. An analogy to Bible translation could be made in this regard.

Some Bible translations strictly follow the original Hebrew and Greek but such very literal renditions can make it difficult to read in other languages. Other translations focus on meaning by reworking sentence structures into a better, native-reading format: a "dynamic equivalent." (*The Chosen Study* uses one slightly tilted toward literal: ESV.)

Still other "translations" paraphrase the original words, or even add interpretation, thus amplifying (but not contradicting) the meaning.

Every film enactment of biblical events falls somewhere on a similar spectrum: from a literal (word-for-word) depiction, to a dynamic equivalent, to a non-literal paraphrase. In the case of *The Chosen*, it would be fair to characterize it as beyond paraphrase to an "amplified version." Some would use this byline under it: *Based on a True Story.*

Such "non-literal," *historical fiction* relies on artistic license, and can cause discomfort which is understandable. If that is true for you, check out the videos by Dallas entitled: *Can you trust The Chosen?* (tinyurl.com/trustthechosen?), as well as an interview with Jonathan Roumie, (tinyurl.com/roumieinterview), who portrays Jesus. These videos convey their perspective and may prove helpful.

We regularly point out what happened versus plausible speculation from *The Chosen*. Ultimately, *The Chosen* is a TV show, and the Bible is the only media inspired by God, given to inform us of the truth and the way things happened. Film brings supportive context and three-dimensional color to the two-dimensional writing on the page.

Dallas' heartfelt, well-achieved mission (see page 17) is why we vigorously support *The Chosen* and have developed *The Chosen Study*.

Background Notes:

More Notes:

Leader's Notes

The Chosen Vision: Dallas and his team share the goal of *reaching a billion people with the message of Jesus.* Our "loaves and fish" effort joins their far-reaching aspirations by **helping study leaders** facilitate **discussions about Jesus with everyone we know, and to see people grow into and as Christ followers.**

If you're on the fence about leading, consider Jesus' challenge to Andrew in Episode 8 of Season One about traveling through the hated Samaritan territory, a place considered unclean and dangerous: *Did you join me for safety reasons?*

So, you're interested in leading a Chosen Study? Here's what to do:

Gather a Core Team

The Chosen Study Team

is a small group with a big purpose.

Draw together a core group made up of those who have seen something "different" in Jesus and want others to experience that difference. The team meets together regularly (shoot for weekly) to support the group process and pray. They plan, oversee the food, and invite friends and family to join in. This team can take on the following roles:

–**The Group Leader** oversees the group's study and discussion process and seeks to foster one-on-one friendship evangelism and discipleship within the group. We encourage the Group Leader to model servant/leadership within the group and to send out weekly emails.

–**The Prayer Team Promoter** finds ways to support the Study in prayer.

–**The Meal Organizer** oversees the food. See *Resources* at the website for theme potluck sign-up sheets. Meal Organizers can also keep in touch during the week with group emails. (The first meal will likely be something like a pizza night instead of a planned potluck.)

–*Child Care Helper* for younger families who need such help to come.

–*Set-Up/Sign-Up/Name Tag/Greeter* should be designated, especially for larger groups. For the people who may not feel comfortable at first, you'll want to extend hospitality and friendship from the start.

–*"Tech Person"* to oversee film presentation and casting to the TV.

–*Small Group Facilitators* (for larger studies—eight or more) oversee their group. **It is best to sit around small tables with just four to six others** (and best to separate spouses), rotating members weekly.

–*Day-Long or Weekend Event Organizer* (see page 15 and the website).

FYI: There are two series. *The Chosen Series* that follows *The Chosen* and *The Bible Series* which includes other film and passage selections from the Gospels and various books of Scripture. (See page 158 and the website for these options.)

Be Inclusive of Everyone

Who to invite? Everyone who is open to come: The religious, the doubters, the non-religious, the seekers—you name it. This is to be a fun, interactive place that values and respects everyone.

We hope group members share differences of opinion and viewpoints from all over the spiritual map. We're glad for that. Each person brings their own background. We're not here to judge. We love to stir up discussion and hear unaccustomed perspectives. As Philip simply said to Nathanael in episode two: *Come and see!*

Sharing and Prayer: To respect where people are spiritually, encourage believers to **avoid insider-type sharing**—which can characterize typical Bible study groups. (Also, prayer should primarily take place before you come/after you leave, not during group time.) A Chosen Study is a **skeptic- and seeker-friendly outreach group** for mutual learning, and to develop deeper friendships both inside and outside the group context.

Get the Word Out

"I feel I've been reading my Bible in black and white all these years and suddenly it's in C-O-L-O-R."

The Chosen Study

A welcoming and interactive experience for everyone: observers...skeptics...learners...seekers...followers.

6-8:45 pm, Tuesdays June 15th to Aug. 17th
Mahonia, Suite #230 / 120 Shelton McMurphey Blvd.

No RSVP—Just Come. For more info: Bill: 541-221-4242
TheChosenStudy.org • DINNER IS PROVIDED

Direct Invitation: Yes, we still do that, right?! Indeed, it is by far the most effective means.

Email Invitation: Get the word out quickly by sending a link to the trailer, website, and a flyer attachment.

Text Invitation: Send out a photo, or better yet, a digital photo (JPG) of your flyer, and an active link to the trailer and website.

Flyers: Contact us at our website to receive sample flyers in MS Word that you can adapt and print or make up your own to hand out.

Create a Facebook Event and **Church Announcements** to the masses.

Once started, keep inviting. New people can binge watch to catch up!

Plan for Food

Our studies seek to connect us to God AND to each other. What better way to bring people together than by sharing food and conversation? We encourage starting with a meal, potluck or, at least, finger food. The role of overseeing the meals is a tremendous service to the group.

Lead/Facilitate the Group

You can begin small—with just one friend, one-on-one, or gather a group. Pray, invite, read, and underline the key points on pages 8-15 and 143-150. The leader's notes along the way, are for both current and future leaders to gain confidence in how to facilitate their groups.

Multiply Your Efforts—through small/large (8+) group combos

Combining small groups within a larger group: When a group starts off large or grows larger—*to eight or more*—the larger size presents unique opportunities. Small groups provide a *depth* of intimacy that allows members to participate more. Larger group interaction can then draw out the best insights from the small group discussions to offer a *breadth* of give-and-take sharing.

This combination **provides for two (shorter) discussion times**, with the best of both dynamics, and gives group leaders the role of a "dialogical" (two-way), not "monological" (one-way), teacher. After each small group time, the leader brings together the larger group for a "check-in" to highlight what was discussed within the small groups.

A small/large group combination **offers a chance for the core team to facilitate the smaller groups**. The goal is to foster a guided conversation. This, likewise, is true for a large group leader on a larger scale. Quality, dialogical teaching brings a soft touch to the group sharing, by focusing on the best insights gleaned from the small groups.

Larger groups thus **provide discipleship opportunities** for group members to step into the role of small group facilitators, as part of the core Chosen Study team. The goal is to help equip an increasing number of these leaders to multiply their outreach efforts in the lives of others. The challenge during the group time is to keep up the pace.

If you're currently a group member with such aspirations, feel free to study through the guide notes, go through the website and look for an opportunity to join a team, or to start your own Chosen Study!

For Leader Support: thechosenstudy.org/join

The website's primary purpose is to equip current and future leaders to make disciples and provide a community of discipleship for those using *The Chosen* for outreach and growth. *How can we serve you?*

Eight Group Ground Rules to Enhance Your Experience

1. *The Leader* is a **facilitator** of discussion, guiding the group through questions rather than statements. He or she is responsible to **prepare for and oversee group interaction** and to **help with outreach.**

2. *The Guide* makes for a valuable personal study but is especially set up to help **current and future leaders** facilitate watching, study, and discussion in one-to-one, and in small/large group settings.

3. *Prior Preparation* though not discouraged, is not expected. We do, however, have a **Home Reflection** time for post-Study follow-up.

4. *Each Group Member* "owns the group," and is thus seen as a key contributor of comments and questions. **Talkative members** should defer to others and **quiet members**, speak out. *The conversation engagement around the circle should look like a pinball machine!*

5. *Group Focus* is controlled by its purpose. *The Chosen* Study allows the episode and Scripture passage to **govern the discussion**, rather than Bible commentaries or cross referencing. Tangents are to be avoided or at least "tabled," until after the group meeting is over.

6. *Personal Growth* from studying Jesus is our goal. Such growth naturally includes a **focus on humility** and **child-like faith.**

7. *Group Growth* happens as **friendships form and deepen.** Members should see themselves as more than just a study group, but as a community where consistency, accountability, self-disclosure, empathy, and reaching out to others are key characteristics.

8. *Avoid making "guest appearances."* Don't let *stay-at-home feelings* or distractions dictate whether you come. **Commit to attend** every meeting. Take this gathering seriously—for you and for others.

Fight "those feelings" and the distractions by signing this challenge:

Unless out-of-town or near death's door, I'll be there: _____

Eight Don'ts of Leading Group Discussions

You're NOT a teacher, you're *a facilitator*. To lead a highly productive group discussion, start with what NOT to do and you're halfway there!

1. Don't answer your own questions. Otherwise, the group will look to you as "the teacher" rather than "the facilitator." You're not just the questioner. You should participate like any member, but don't be the first one to answer your own question.

2. Don't over-talk. Groups with an overtalkative leader will often sit back—in boredom! 90% of what we hear we forget, but 90% of what we say, we remember. So, your goal is to get your group talking. Get them remembering. Get them learning.

3. Don't be afraid of silence. Silence may mean you need to rephrase the question, but if you "bail out your group" when silent, you set a bad precedent. To exercise patience, count in your head from 100 to 0 before answering—then, only if you must. Oh, yes, they'll talk!

4. Don't be content with just one answer. For every written question feel free to ask a follow-up question or two, like: "Does anyone else have a thought?" This allows several people to respond.

5. Don't expect group members to respond with an answer each time. They'll be tempted to look straight at you solely, especially when the group is new. Instead, you want them talking to each other, so you don't have to be the "discussion hub" (see page 150).

6. Don't reject an answer as wrong. Respond to questionable answers by asking, "How did you come to that conclusion?" or "There's probably a difference of opinion here. Does anyone else have another way of looking at this?" Be affirming to everyone.

7. Don't be afraid of controversy. Different opinions are a good thing.

8. Don't allow the group to end late. If the discussion proves fruitful, end on time. Don't let the group drag on, but for those who choose to stay, give opportunity to discuss the issue in more depth.

Eight Do's of Leading Group Discussions

You don't need to be an expert or trained teacher to lead a discussion group. Your role is that of a **facilitator**, one who guides the group into a productive conversation that centers on the episodes' and studies' main points. It's an honor to be able to serve your group in this way.

1. **Bring along your own curiosity and have fun with it.** Good start!

2. **Pace the study.** It's the leader's responsibility to both start and end on time. Keep up a flexible pace with one eye on the clock and the other on the content. There may be more questions than you have time for; so, if necessary, skip some questions. Press ahead!

3. **Give members the chance to study on their own.** They are free to do so—or not. There is no expectation of prior preparation.

4. **Have the Scripture passage read aloud.** Ask a member to read. Some may feel uncomfortable reading in public, so don't make "surprise assignments," unless you know they're willing to do so.

5. **Be on alert for over talkative people.** Someone who over-talks can squeeze the life out of a group. If this is a problem, engage with the group member after the meeting, and enlist their help to join you in the goal of getting everyone involved in the discussion.

6. **Involve everyone, more or less equally.** Sit across from quiet people to draw them out, and next to talkative people to make less eye contact. If helpful, go around the circle with a question.

7. **Keep the discussion on track by avoiding tangents**. Tangents may seem important but can hurt purposeful discussion, leading the group to talk about less important things. "Important tangents" provide opportunities for conversation outside the group's time.

8. **Conduct a discussion first with general, then specific questions.** Your goal is NOT to get into one-and-done responses; rather, your goal is to start a engaging dialogue with several people responding to a particular question in a back-and-forth way (see the next page).

Monological vs. Dialogical Interaction

If tables (small round or rectangle) are available, they are preferred for the meals and for group study (of ideally four to six participants each).

Dialogical interaction engages wide-ranging participation. Such give-and-take discussion sparked by the *table leader* and the *up-front leader* is desired. **Interaction from a leader's question is visualized below:**

Inferior Monological Interaction   Superior Dialogical Interaction

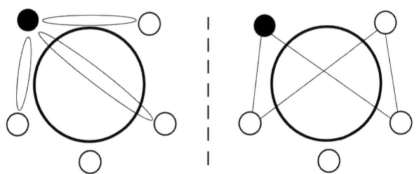

Small/Larger Group Combination—Can Work with Eight or More

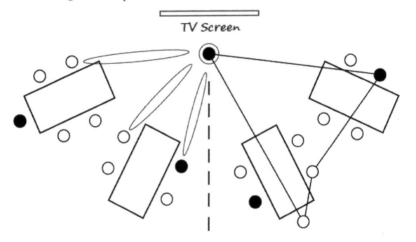

TV Screen

Dialogical leading *facilitates interaction* among your group members, and limits *brokering their discussion* seen above. As a leader you can participate, but your goal is to get others talking. 90% of what you say they'll forget, but 90% of what you get them to say, they'll remember!

Leader's Notes: What applies most to you and your group?

-

-

-

-

-

-

-

-

-

-

-

-

-

-

-

-

Your Chosen Group: Names, info., prayer concerns, etc.

-
-
-
-
-
-
-
-
-
-
-
-
-
-
-
-

Your Chosen Group: Names, info., prayer concerns, etc.

-
-
-
-
-
-
-
-
-
-
-
-
-
-
-

Note: For a sign-up sheet to print off, see the website under *Resources*.

Leader's Notes:

Our Mission: What We're About

The Chosen Study combines film depiction with Scripture
study in a welcoming and interactive experience for all:
observers... skeptics... learners... seekers... followers,
who WATCH > DISCUSS > RELATE together
the Most Audacious Story ever told.

Our Executive Leadership Team: What We Do

We work with Chosen Study Leaders, helping them succeed at gathering people, creating a friendly place and a compelling means to talk about Jesus.

Back to Front, Left to Right:
Bill Ditewig, Dietrich Gruen, Bill & Teresa Syrios and Cathy & Don Baker

Our Invitation: Start a Group–Join the Team–Zoom with Us

Do you have some loaves and fish to bring to this endeavor? We are looking for those who have seen "the Jesus' difference" and are interested in exploring how to spread that difference around the world using The Chosen Study. If that sounds like you, contact us: thechosenstudy.org/join or facebook.com/thechosenstudy.

More Notes:

Order Guides (with volume discount): thechosenstudy.org/order

The Chosen Study: **Season One,** focuses on Simon, Matthew, Andrew, Nicodemus, and Mary Magdalene as they encounter Jesus. This guide, based on the hugely popular show, *The Chosen,* will give you and your group an in-depth appreciation of their unexpected changes of fortune in getting to know him.

The Chosen Study: **Season Two,** guides you and your group into Act Two of Jesus' life and ministry with his followers unsure of where all this is going.

Here we meet the remaining disciples, such as Nathanael, who is despondent over a career in shambles, only to be given a new vocation by Jesus. Besides him, there are a host of others with physical, mental, and emotional infirmities, even demon-possession that, up to now, have been impossible to overcome.

The Chosen Study: **Season Three,** will begin with *The Messengers*—which first aired in theaters before Christmas, 2021. It then picks up where season two ended, with the famous *Sermon on the Mount.*

Chosen seasons four through seven

We know little of what's coming, other than season six will focus on Jesus' crucifixion and season seven, his resurrection. Otherwise, stay tuned for many more gospel stories!

Special one-time Chosen event

***The Messengers,* Christmas Special:** This episode can be used as a *come-one-come-all event* for your group or church before Christmas. Some are more open spiritually around Christmas. Watching and discussing this episode could act as a winter-quarter (January) kickoff for a new Chosen group. To access it, see: tinyurl.com/chosen-messengers

Further encouragement

***The Chosen:* 40 Days with Jesus** provides a new devotional for each season to extend your experience throughout the week. You can space it out to follow a five-a-week schedule. Order at Amazon or bookstores.

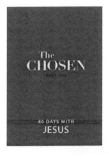

Divide the 40 devotional readings into five readings per week.

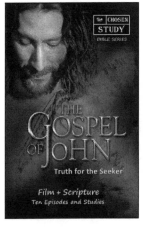

Bible Series

We're spoiled by *The Chosen,* but there are other quality, biblical movies, and *Jesus films* out there. Here's one that we are working on:

The John Study is a ten-week study based on a film entitled *The Life of Jesus.* This three-hour movie is a word-for-word portrayal of John's Gospel from the *Good News Bible* translation.

Here's the movie: tinyurl.com/the-john-film

Manuscript Bible Study

We use four-color BIC pens to colorfully study biblical texts in a simple *Mark-It-Up* style.

The *M-I-U format* is based on something more in-depth called *manuscript Bible study*.

Such study is done on 8 ½ x 11" sheets. The text is set out with margins as seen in this example from the first 15 verses of Mark's Gospel.

For more info and to access downloadable manuscripts: manuscriptbiblestudy.com.

How to Lead and Promote a Chosen Study

The Chosen Study really began on May 28, 2021, with a Zoom call between Bill Syrios and some gifted Bible study leaders. Get in on that call here: tinyurl.com/how-to-lead. Also, learn to lead in the process!

Let's do this thing!

The Chosen Study Zoom calls continued, led by Bill, with some new-found colleagues. These calls, on June 4 and 11, 2021, focus on promoting your Chosen group to others. See: tinyurl.com/lead-and-promote.

Final Thoughts!

Made in the USA
Monee, IL
13 February 2023

27759783R00090